10-8-63   (62-13731)

Power and Stability
in Nigeria

POWER AND STABILITY
IN NIGERIA

THE POLITICS OF DECOLONIZATION

HENRY L. BRETTON

FREDERICK A. PRAEGER, *Publisher*
New York

BOOKS THAT MATTER

First published in the United States of America in 1962 by
Frederick A. Praeger, Inc., Publisher
64 University Place, New York 3, N.Y.

Manufactured in the United States of America

To the memory of

W. W. S.

Preface

This book addresses itself to the politics of decolonization in a newly independent African country. Such an effort may be long overdue, although there are, to be sure, a number of excellent books on government and politics in developing countries. Of the books on Nigeria, Coleman's *Nigeria: Background to Nationalism*[1] must be considered the most valuable and most significant study so far. However, most of the articles and books about Nigeria, and about British Africa generally, fall far short of shedding light on the problem there. The majority, including many so-called "scholarly" studies, suffer from political astigmatism; for although they are often profusely documented, they merely paraphrase official reports prepared by diplomatically trained members of the European or African bureaucracy, whose purpose it is to conceal rather than to reveal. No real insights should be expected, for example, from studies of elections and electoral conduct in Nigeria if most of the information derives from official records and reports. Finally, there are those students of African affairs whose astigmatism stems from their sincere but overwhelming love and concern for the people of the long-abused and exploited "dark continent."

The study of African politics, like that of all developing areas, requires methods that may in many respects appear to be unorthodox, especially to the student of European politics, for instance. The difficulties have been discussed more fully elsewhere,[2] but I should like to stress the fact that special problems arise because environmental and procedural conditions in the developing areas differ significantly from those characteristic of advanced societies. The problems are compounded not only of the normal consequences of social, economic, psychological, and political variables, but also of the special shock effects of change characteristic of the latter part of the twentieth century. Under such conditions, governmental and political processes do not, as in more advanced areas, represent static, readily identifiable forces and interests; rather, they tend to defy neat and convenient type-casting and classifications.

The strictly historical and institutional approach to the analytical study of government and politics may be considered inappropriate for the study of developing areas because the constitutional and formal aspects of their political systems rarely outlive the writing, printing, and publishing of the constitutional documents themselves. Frequently, what scholars may still be gravely pondering or discussing in sweeping generalizations may have already been superseded, in practice, by arrangements more in line with the prevailing distribution of power. If, at times, some constitutional documents, and the instrumentalities derived therefrom, appear to survive their publication, the reason is, more often than not, that they have by then already been reduced to mummified existence: Life and soul have long departed. Thus, because in Africa today political reality quickly outstrips formal structural and institutional arrangements, this political analysis of Nigeria treats formal aspects solely as background material of secondary importance.

The broad outlines of this study, substantially altered and adapted to African conditions where necessary, are derived from Lasswell and Kaplan, *Power and Society,*[3] a work that attempts to provide a more effective tool for political analysis—more effective, that is, than the traditional, predominantly descriptive method, which, of necessity, has to be confined primarily to available documentation on the "visible," formal, institutional, and structural aspects of government and politics. A basic assumption underlying *Power and Society* is that the essence of the political process is concealed rather than revealed by the formal side of the system. The author apologizes to Lasswell and Kaplan for the free use to which their *"framework for inquiry"* has been put; the responsibility for the consequences of such use, and, incidentally, for everything else in this book, is the author's.

The raw data upon which the present study is based were compiled, in part, during several years of study of government and politics in Africa, including field trips to Nigeria and to Great

Britain in 1956, 1957, 1959, and 1962. Much of the substantive information, and many of the insights, was obtained directly from
Nigerian and European officials, political leaders, and private individuals, frequently on a confidential basis. At the risk of giving
the study an "unscholarly" appearance, I have kept source references to a minimum. At the present stage in the development of
literature on African politics, an open-ended analysis, paying only
limited attention to official documents, yet not sacrificing the scholarly intent, seemed to me to have value. Therefore, although I have
consulted relevant materials, I have concentrated on a statement
of problems and of problem-complexes, rather than a meticulous
but politically unrealistic account of formal structural arrangements. In 1957, for example, I had occasion to talk to an official
in the Ministry of France Overseas several months after the extensive *Loi Cadre,* which was to recast the legal-constitutional
structure in the French overseas possessions, had been published.
At the very moment that numerous ponderous commentaries on
this apparently significant document were being prepared and
published, the French official woefully conceded that the *Loi
Cadre* already had become obsolete.

I gratefully acknowledge the funds made available in support
of publication by the Board of Governors of the Horace H. Rack-
ham School of Graduate Studies, funds which are derived from
the endowment of the School. Equally appreciated is the assistance granted by the Whiting Foundation. Acknowledgment is
also due to the Begole Brownell Fund of the Department of Political Science of the University of Michigan for partial assistance
toward the typing of the manuscript, and to Leonard W. Doob and
Samuel J. Eldersveld, who contributed to certain projects related
to the present study from their National Academy of Science and
Ford Foundation grants, respectively. Not to be forgotten are
the sacrifices made by my wife, without which the field trips, and
the preparation of this book, would not have been possible.

Some of my numerous Nigerian and European friends and ac-
quaintances, whose assistance and advice are hereby acknowl-

edged, may find parts of the present study difficult to accept. I wish to express my conviction, however, that when they are unburdened of momentary emotional attachments, ideological commitments, or other motivational impediments, they will recognize the essential need for the kind of critique offered here, or implied, in the interest of the advancement of Nigeria as a whole.

H. L. B.

The University of Michigan
Ann Arbor, Michigan
February 15, 1962

Contents

Power and Stability
in Nigeria

Introduction

The main focus of this study is upon political stability as a most critical factor in decolonization. By political stability, I refer to a state of affairs that permits a political system to function without subjection to political changes not in accordance with the accepted and established rules or formulas. Nigeria has been selected for such a study because it is the largest and most populous African state and because the fate of all Africa may hinge on its survival. In terms of its potential power and influence, Nigeria may become the most important country in the African continent, and as a political anchor for a system of free African states, Nigeria could be invaluable.

It may, of course, be argued that political stability depends, in turn, on economic factors and forces. The present study is based on the premise, however, that especially in the poorer societies of the world, economic development takes place under the general control and supervision of political forces, that substantive and directional choices are made on political grounds, and that generally, in the decolonization process, the political "kingdom" precedes the economic one. Hence, regardless of theoretical merits of a given economic development program, the achievement of social stability depends initially, during the most critical stages, on the ability of the post-independence political system to weather the storms released by decolonization. Therefore, in the present context, political stability is treated as the most critical, vital, and fundamental aspect in terms of Nigeria's national survival.

Although, in strictly legal terms, Nigeria's accession to independence on October 1, 1960, warranted special notice—since a legal transfer of some aspects of power did indeed take place then —in terms of real, substantive political power and control, and of economic power and influence, the event lacked the significance popularly attributed to it. Under the conditions worked out between British and Nigerian interests, extensive preparation had been made for the transfer of governmental and administrative responsibilities to the Nigerians on a piecemeal basis. True self-government had been brought to the territory several years before formal independence was granted—first to the southern, then to the northern parts; consequently, many of the lesser attributes of rule had already been transferred, and others, it was mutually agreed, did not have to be transferred immediately. Economic and military powers, for instance, were substantially retained by the British in one form or another, and the Nigerians, because of a rather delicate internal political balance, found such a "staggering" of the processes of power transfer politically convenient. Thus, it cannot be said that October 1, 1960, saw the emergence of a brand-new political regime in Nigeria or of brand-new political patterns and relationships. The roots of government were not torn up on independence day, nor were entirely new roots planted. Therefore, a valid examination of Nigeria's political processes must take into account the presence of the British before, during, and for some time after independence.* Furthermore, assuming that Nigeria will abruptly and radically alter neither her relationship to Great Britain nor the basic structure of the political-legal system inherited from the colonial mother country, one can say that, initially, at least, the rulers of independent Nigeria will be the inheritors of political and legal doctrines that are predominantly Western. The system under which Nigeria will be ruled is thus nonindigenous, the result of interaction between European colonial and indigenous rulers who have entered into some kind of compact and arrived at some agreement concerning institutional and procedural outlines of government.

* Because Nigerian-British relations were formally altered as a result of the legal transfer of power, that subject could perhaps properly be considered under the heading of foreign relations. Actually, under the circumstances, relations between the two countries have an intrinsic bearing on political stability in Nigeria. If relations between the two countries were to be subjected to the strains that characterized Franco-Guinean relations at the moment of independence, Nigeria would be shaken to its foundations.

On the other hand, it must be considered a distinct possibility that relations between Great Britain and Nigeria will be subjected to multiple strains and stresses—although not necessarily severe or shocking—from the resulting legal transfer of power and all that it entails. Therefore, neither the philosophy nor the operation of the system, jointly constructed, can be predetermined by its creators. As soon as power and responsibility have been transferred in substance—and it has been pointed out that the terminal date is being deferred well beyond independence day—the African rulers will have to fall back upon their own resources to resist the usual internal pressures related to the struggle for power itself and for the rights and privileges associated with positions of power and influence. In fact, as soon as such positions have been sufficiently increased in value as a result of the accrual of power, the struggle will become intensified. Then drastic political change will become more worth while because the stakes will be higher; and the political system will be subjected to increased pressures toward the creation of conditions that will facilitate a new transfer of power.

Because these conditions are likely to become permanent features of Nigerian politics for the foreseeable future, it is of course to be expected that forces and factors tending to create, or work toward the creation of, political instability will outweigh, for some time to come, the stabilizing factors. Nigerian society will most likely be increasingly subjected to revolutionary pressures strong enough to warrant the application of repressive and even punitive measures by the rulers.* In such a setting, democratic values receive a relatively low operational priority in ruling circles except as covering myths, and mechanical, legal and philosophical aspects of the democratic system tend to be disregarded.

* "Revolutionary," as used here, refers to a state of affairs in which the rule, or the system, is being effectively challenged by internal forces or in which the rule would be effectively challenged and eventually overthrown if free play were permitted all contending forces, or at least those capable of establishing a counterrule.

Part One

THE COLONIAL BEQUEST:
IMPEDIMENTA OR BLESSINGS?

The Roots of the Prevailing System

Preparation for What?

The legal framework for this analysis is provided by the 1960 constitutional document, as amended up to now, and by evidence of understandings and arrangements concerning the operation of the formal system by the partners to the transfer of power. The social structure is that of pre-independence—in some areas, pre-colonial—days. The key control points in the economy, in the military and police machinery, and in the judicial and political branches were developed in their present form by the colonial rulers and taken over—not always, however, in significant respects—by Nigerian elite elements with the active assistance and the full political blessing, in most instances, of the colonial power. In this connection, it should be understood that the legal-political framework within which the political processes take place was developed by the British rulers in part to assure, as far as it was possible and feasible, some degree of continuing control and influence after the legal and formal separation. Thus, at times, where the Nigerian environment is discussed, one may actually still be dealing with substantially unaltered British-instituted structural or procedural aspects rather than with an indigenous variant of the British system. As the transfer of power is extended, however, this factor will be less in evidence, and exclusively Nigerian and African environmental factors will become dominant.

The power struggle in Nigeria differs significantly from that recorded in other parts of the world at earlier periods. Therefore, anyone who attempts to make analogies must take care, for in a country such as Nigeria the results may be wholly unpredictable.

A survey of the more recent history of Nigeria, particularly in regard to the power structure, produces the following picture. In the north, the structure appears to have been most decisively influenced and shaped by the region's proximity to the sources of Islamic civilization and its relative remoteness from the areas ravaged by slave-raiding. Before the arrival of British forces in the Northern Region, quasi-oriental systems of despotism, some of the "great Sudanese empires," had been developed there. These systems showed sufficient social and political cohesiveness to obviate excessive intervention by the Europeans in native affairs. The social discipline primarily derived from Islam produced adequate stability and seemed to provide more effective means of law enforcement and general administration than direct British intervention could have achieved at the time. Lord Hailey observes that the larger political units in the north featured "a well-organized fiscal system, a definitive code of land tenure, a regular scheme of local rule through appointed district heads, and a trained judiciary administering the tenets of Mohammedan law."[1] Under the circumstances, the colonial rulers had an incentive to confirm those of the northern feudal aristocracy who were willing to accept the British "protectorate." The indigenous power structure could be made an integral part of colonial rule, and of the exploitative schemes associated with that rule, without incisive revolutionary changes imposed from outside. The local-government system, termed "indirect rule" at one stage, merely legitimized the local power structure.

Social and political stability in the north, then, was largely the result of British acquiescence in the continuation of an inherently stable feudal system of government. The traditional rulers, who derived their internal legitimacy from theocratic sources, exercised nearly total control over the land and other sources of wealth, including both the existing and potential channels of commercial distribution. Hierarchical problems of rule and succession were settled through relatively well-established procedures. So, too, were the problems related to the recruitment of new leadership material. Very few families were involved in native rule at the more significant levels, and claims to positions of power and prestige were not too diversified. Circumstances made it relatively easy for the colonial rulers to assist in the solution of hierarchical or succession conflicts in a discreet, unobtrusive manner. Political rewards and punishments could be applied without serious political repercussions.

In the southern parts of the country, a number of physical and social factors operated through the centuries of potential and actual contact with Islam and Christianity to produce different power structures and diverse political processes and customs. The dense tropical forest and the tsetse fly, among other factors, appear to have served as a barrier to the southward march of Islam, at least for a time. In this relative isolation from vigorous and aggressive outside influences, prior to the European intrusion, several well-organized and effective political units emerged, particularly in the Western Region among the Yoruba and Edo.[2] Geographic and social factors combined to produce heavy urban concentrations with their resultant political configurations. After contact with European civilization was established, the southern sections were intensively subjected to the processes of acculturation, primarily in the wake of missionary and trading activities. Slaving affected the social and spiritual fabric of the coastal areas only in a negative way—unless the growth of the indigenous middle class with its slave-trading antecedents is considered a positive factor—and much of the degeneration encountered in certain sections must be traced to that cause. Generally, factors tending to produce social and political stability were counteracted by agencies associated with colonial exploitation. The power structure in the southern sections was rendered pliable, to the benefit of the Europeans, by the historic and periodic assaults to which the areas closest to the landing and intrusion points were exposed.

The eastern sections of Nigeria, primarily for geographic reasons, experienced greater social fractionalization than either the north or the west. Dense forests, as in certain parts of early Europe,

discouraged centralization. And one significant factor in the east
has been the virtual absence of the kind of large-scale, vigorous
empires that had developed in the north or of such relatively
cohesive and large-scale organizations as were found among the
Yoruba and Edo in the west.

In all three instances, the intention of British administrative
policy apparently was to make the predominant power structure
and underlying social systems compatible with the requirements
of colonial rule. British control over traditional rulers was exercised through either the conferral or denial of legitimacy status.
Traditional systems were either recognized or repudiated according to the utility value of the system to colonial—primarily economic—exploitation. The acceptance of the "Queen's peace" meant
subordination and integration; a challenge to the new order meant
swift intervention by the colonial rulers. Such intervention ranged
from the direct removal of obstreperous tribal dignitaries, or of a
group of key men in the traditional power structure, to military or
economic disciplinary action and the imposition of penalties. The
threat of banishment to remote regions—or even of actual depor-
tation—also served as a warning to potentially or actually unco-
operative leaders. Most important, perhaps, was the fact that
no indigenous leader was permitted to become a member of the
inner circle of manipulators of supreme political power. No matter how laden with titles and honors, indigenous rulers operated
on the periphery of the essential power struggle, without being
at all involved in the determination of major policies. Theirs was a
purely subsidiary role.

Once the European rulers had decided that some power had to
be transferred, they preferred to transfer it to the *legitimized* (i.e.,
the accepted) traditional rulers. In defense of that approach,
they asserted that if representatives of the mass parties, for instance—usually younger men with little experience in government
—were to be placed in positions of responsibility, they would
surely lead the country into chaos and destruction. Actually, it
was the traditional ruler who, more often than not, was unquali-

fied for modern government and, more important, frequently lacked the intellectual capacity for leadership. There were, however—and still are—outstanding exceptions to that rule.

For a variety of reasons, traditional regimes proved *a priori* more susceptible to large-scale and widespread corruption, mismanagement, and intrigue than secular, modern systems. If modern democratic self-government was the goal, no elements were less suitable to the development of such a system than the traditional rulers and their retinue. As it turned out, however, developments elsewhere, both inside and outside the Empire and Commonwealth, caused future plans to be drastically altered during the 1950's. The train carrying the chiefs and elders into the future, as well-subsidized bearers of colonial authority, suddenly had to be shunted onto a siding to make room for the fast express of nationalism. Under the circumstances, the phenomenon of continued British association and identification with the new rulers, however tenuous such identification may in reality be, remains an eloquent testimonial to British colonial statecraft and diplomatic skill.

Many of the less well-educated chiefs were at a loss to explain the new policy. They could not understand why the British, seemingly committed to their support, would so soon want to withdraw that support in favor of upstarts. They could not appreciate, of course, the predicament that now confronted colonialism as a result of the social revolution sweeping the continent.

But in many ways, the British contributed, voluntarily as well as involuntarily, to the growth and development of the very nationalism that they had sought for so long to contain through the medium of traditional rule. Of considerable consequence were the pressures from British Labour circles, which were, in turn, encouraged and supported by anticolonialists in North America and the Soviet Union. Further influence was exerted by leaders from formerly colonial territories, particularly Asians, and more and more pressure was being applied by the United Nations and related agencies. And, of course, such pressures were materially helped along by the political and economic consequences of two world wars, by scientific and technological advances in production and distribution methods, and by revolutionary developments in communications, transportation, and other fields.

Still, the old leaders were useful as spiritual and temporal rulers in the traditional, tribal setting; but they could not have survived politically without outside support. They could not, for example, have retained traditional systems and institutions in the face of ever more pressing demands for social and technological change. Thus, in the north, primarily as a matter of mutual survival and the attainment of common goals, a community of interests took shape that tied the traditional elite ever more firmly to the colonial regime. The native rulers became, in fact, defenders of the colonial status quo.

Now, here and there an individual traditional ruler—either because he happens to enjoy the advice of a competent and far-sighted local representative of the colonial regime or of educated and intelligent African counsellors or because he recognizes the handwriting on the wall—adjusts himself to the modern secular system in his area of authority. Frequently, this leads to pathetic results: The royal quarters are swept; corrupt practices are superficially covered up; some messengers and minor officials are disciplined; and the chief takes an apparent interest in a school, a road, a hospital, a bridge. For the sake of appearances, he becomes progressive, but probably he does not understand or perceive the implications of what he is doing. When he does obtain a glimpse of the future, he visualizes the demise of the world of which he is a part; hence, he tends to resist change far more than he tends to adjust.

Thus, as independence nears and is granted, conditions rapidly outpace the interests and capabilities of traditional rulers. The social, economic, and technological forces that are generated are, on the whole, dysfunctional to the traditional regimes and systems, for unknown techniques are applied, new concepts are introduced in a setting compounded of unknown factors and of forces not yet in operation. Moreover, the direction in which that society is moving is to a considerable extent determined by events that occur not in Nigeria but in China, the Soviet Union, India, or at the United Nations, by alien culture influences, by the wholly unfathomable crosscurrents of African international politics. Therefore, a society not yet very mobile, not yet socially integrated beyond the local, cellular units, is set in motion psychologically and spiritually. It is stimulated by alien ideas and practices; it is involved ideologically before its people are involved socially.

Thus the suggestion might be warranted that conditions governing the power struggle in a country like Nigeria differ sharply and substantially from those under which European countries ironed out their problems over the centuries—problems such as those of church, labor, socialism, capitalism, feudalism, the military, aristocracy, etc. Crosscurrents of world politics, ideological warfare, economic competition, and military-strategic pressures affect the development of a country like Nigeria with shock effects. New dimensions of environmental analysis are required to do justice to the Nigerian experience.

For our present purpose, little of value for the study of politics can be extracted from the mass of literature on Nigeria, not only because of the built-in bias of all European, African, or, in general, all white ethnocentric coverage but because of a serious lack of appreciation among most commentators and observers of social, political, and cultural dynamics of development and its attendant effects.

Political Philosophy of Transition

The prevailing political system in its *formal respects* is Anglo-Saxon in origin, but not in substance and application. The system may be described more accurately as colonial democracy—that is, a mixture of authoritarian and nominally democratic rule. The system springs from combinations of several factors: African aristocratic and traditional rule, the effects of Western economic exploitative interests and practices, Western precepts of correct political behavior, the requirements of imperial diplomatic tactics concerning the form and mode of transfer of power, and such mechanistic requirements of formal democracy as elections and parliaments. The system is of a makeshift nature, more improvised than is generally acknowledged by its defenders; it has evolved under great pressure, roughly in the space of ten years or less. The legal and conceptual foundations were laid in the British Colonial Office, and in a few places nearby; secondary aspects were added by British overseas personnel and African leaders and by other European and African organized interests. From the British point of view, the legal-constitutional system has value primarily in terms of the future relations between the two countries, and with regard to such group interests as those of the expatriate bureaucracy and the commercial and military elements. The system lacks intrinsic philosophic value or orientation. Actually, British governments are not permanently committed to the system, not even for the sake of the Commonwealth, and will accept fundamental changes, but preferably only if satisfactory alternatives can be worked out.

The African political leaders and groups likewise lack a vested interest and long-range commitment to the formal aspects of the system, except insofar as the opportunities for pressure politics, which are part of Western democracy, tend to aid them in the power struggle prior to and during the first years of independence. There is only the most tenuous philosophic link between the system as introduced by Britain and the ideological values and perspectives shared by African traditional and modern rulers. There are no philosophic links between the substantive historic past of Nigeria and the modern legal-constitutional system under which the country now operates. In fact, Western democracy never really operated in any colonial areas; instead, the substantially altered modes of government and administration that did operate were far more traditional and far more authoritarian than appeared to be permissible under the provisions of the formal structure.

On the strength of a series of interviews conducted by the writer, the following hypothesis appears to be justified: Any attachment to modern, Western democratic principles professed by Nigerian leaders and opinion-makers may be extremely superficial. In fact, the slightest ideological push, the application of the slightest counterstimulant, reveals, in most instances, a total lack of comprehension of the implications of personal political conduct, under conditions of democracy. Thus, while some overt manifestations of contemporary Nigerian political thought can be superficially traced primarily to British and French, and only secondarily to North American sources, the attachment to the concepts underlying the legal-constitutional system does not appear to be of sufficient intensity and depth to withstand the inevitable pressure from opposing and perhaps socially more attractive—because more relevant—or more rewarding ideas or systems. It is likely that a first step will be the abandonment of the remaining vestiges of the British monarchy in favor of a republican form of government.

2

Westminster: Export Model

On Paper

The formal structure of a society is as stable and as permanent as fundamental social-economic and political conditions warrant. If the formal structure does not adequately reflect the real power structure, or if the two are at odds, the formal structure will be adjusted until it does either correspond with the actual power structure or at least does not impede manipulation of the instruments of power by the real and effective rulers. The Westminster model, even insofar as it has been adapted to Nigerian conditions, clearly does not reflect either the real power structure or the one about to emerge, and it will, therefore, be subjected to alterations until it does become suitable. It would thus serve no useful purpose to go into great detail regarding the constitutional-legal structure in operation at the time of writing. Briefly and summarily described, the prevailing constitutional setup is as follows:

The Federation of Nigeria at present consists of three regions —the Northern, Eastern, and Western—and the Federal Territory of Lagos. Under the colonial regime, these territories were gradually moved toward federation by following staggered periods of self-government, during which selected executive, legislative, judicial, and administrative functions were transferred, at least nominally, into Nigerian hands. For reasons already stated, the Northern Region was permitted to lag behind in every respect; there the social structure was quite incompatible with modern legal and political concepts, institutions, and processes. Even if universal franchise alone had been effectively applied, it would have produced revolutionary situations that neither the British nor their partners in the southern parts of the territory were prepared

18

to handle. At the time of independence, therefore, Nigeria represented a federal organism that accorded the Northern Region distinctly differential treatment, permitting the Islamic feudal rulers of the north to retain their supreme positions subject only to modest restrictions imposed in the common Nigerian interest—"interest" in that sense being rather narrowly interpreted in favor of retaining the status quo.

A bicameral legislature (Parliament), located in Lagos and consisting of the House of Representatives and the Senate, constitutes the legislative apex of the federal structure. Members of the House are elected in single-member constituencies on a population basis. Members of the Senate are selected, twelve from each region, with the approval of the respective regional legislatures. Additional senators are appointed to represent the Federal Territory of Lagos and the federal government as such. A Federal Council of Ministers is formed by the Federal Prime Minister, who, in turn, is appointed by the Governor-General. The latter, as long as the British monarchy is accepted, acts for the Queen in a manner corresponding to the Queen's functions in the British setting. He lacks effective powers, however, for he possesses only stand-by powers that are to be employed when and if needed in the interest of national survival. The effective directing authority at the executive level is vested in the office of the Federal Prime Minister; constitutionally, he is ultimately responsible for law and order, for the administration of the federation, and for the conduct of defense and foreign relations.*

As in the case of the Westminster model, the House of Representatives, equivalent in a very broad sense to the House of Commons, constitutes the formal source of legislative authority. The

---

* Under the prevailing system, exercise of the sensitive function of Commander-in-Chief is the nominal prerogative of the Governor-General. In practice, however, the Federal Prime Minister appears to be his effective rival. One of the key problems to be resolved before Nigeria becomes a Republic concerns the relative positions of the President of the Republic and the Federal Prime Minister with regard to effective control of the Armed Forces, especially in the event of riot or insurrection.

Senate, very roughly corresponding to the British House of Lords, is a reflection largely of traditional rule and is nonpartisan—in the strict sense of that term—in its political makeup. The federal government is not responsible to it, and the decisions of the Senate on bills can be overridden, under certain conditions, by the lower House.

The regional governments likewise have bicameral legislatures, each consisting of a house of assembly and a house of chiefs. All members of the houses of assembly are elected, but special conditions apply in the north. As at the federal level, the regional lower houses represent the primary and dominant sources of legislative authority, and the houses of chiefs reflect the traditional rule and interests associated with it. Executive councils, consisting of premiers and ministers, are responsible to the respective houses of assembly for the conduct of governmental affairs and the administration of the regions. Governors represent the Queen or the Governor-General in each region; they nominate and appoint the premiers with a view to their ability to command majorities in the respective assemblies. These parliamentary and ministerial systems developed gradually after the introduction of the Macpherson Constitution in 1951.

All legislative, executive, and judicial bodies are, of course, relatively inexperienced. Many of the powers allocated to them under the federal scheme cannot be wielded effectively. Nominally, the regional governments are allocated reserved powers in the fields of health, agriculture, and education (except for higher education); they share with the federal government concurrent powers concerning trade, labor, industrial development, roads, prisons, and public works. Exclusive powers are granted the federal government in the spheres of external affairs and defense, banks and banking, basic communications, etc. The Senate, guardian-designate of regional interests, is far too inexperienced a body to carry out its constitutional assignment effectively; however, on at least one occasion, toward the end of 1961, the Senate did act to prevent a change in the constitution of the Northern Region that could have strengthened the north to the disadvantage of the rest of the country.[1] Mutual suspicions, the preoccupation of the relatively backward Northern Region with its own development, and the rivalry among the several leading regional politicians interfere significantly with the proper workings of the federal system. The mass of representatives in the several houses cannot for some time to come generate the political efforts required to lend substance to their nominal legislative prerogatives and powers. Under the circumstances, it is only a temporary phenomenon that the system appears to be headed for stability, largely the result of operations of extraconstitutional factors. In the north, for instance, the feudal structure is the *sine qua non* of stability; without it, the parliamentary structure would surely have become wholly inoperative as soon as it was established. Elsewhere, much depends on the role the remaining British civil servants are permitted to play during the critical years of developing a workable, durable constitutional structure. Much depends, too, on the continued operation of other British improvements in the economy and in society generally before new formal institutions can begin to move the country toward more stable conditions.

In a federal system, the allocation of revenue to the several component parts is of crucial importance, partly because of its potentialities as an instrument of control and coercion. If employed wisely, it could have stabilizing effects; but under the Nigerian scheme, the greatest share of the total federal revenue is collected by the federal government through import and export duties and income tax. A substantial share of such revenue is then reallocated to the regions, and it provides the principal source of revenue for the operation of the regional governments. Taylor Cole points out that "well over one-half of the regional revenue is thus derived from the federal grants and allocations to the regions."[2] However, the "infrastructure"—that is, the fundamental economic, administrative, and political-social structures—is not developed sufficiently to permit the application of fiscal-regulatory powers of the federal government to political regulation and stabilization in the several regions. Although agreements have been reached (in limited areas) on such matters as transportation, for instance, Nigeria still appears to be a considerable distance from the realization of the functional goals laid down in the formal constitutional framework given at the time of independence.

In Practice

On the surface, the formal constitutional framework under which Nigeria attained independence might have appeared flexible enough to permit compromise, adjustment, and change. It seemed loose enough to accommodate a multitude of conflicting groups, especially those with fundamentally different concepts of government and administration; and it seemed permissive enough to facilitate progressive methods of personnel recruitment, to allow changes within the governing bodies, and to accommodate opposing views in government. In actual operational terms, however, the framework served merely as a model. Its primary function was to set the guidelines for constitutional development and, perhaps most important, to facilitate the transference of power under conditions which, in the absence of such a model, would have tended to render unified administration of the territory highly problematic, if not impossible. In short, it was a makeshift device.

In a setting such as Nigeria, the Westminster model, even with federalist modifications, actually is a source of weakness rather than of strength. It may have served well during the earlier periods when it operated in a typically colonial fashion—that is, as an authoritarian version of the original model; but then it served the interests of the alien rulers, not those of the indigenous people. And it worked reasonably well primarily because the political conditions under which the model operated had, of course, never been transferred from the mother country. But as new African interests develop, with correspondingly greater African representation at the top levels of government and administration, its alien origin will render the Westminster model more and more embarrassing, perhaps even repugnant, and pressures will mount to replace it with a system more closely corresponding to local tastes and requirements. Suspicions will mount that the alien model was left behind as a kind of legal trap, or Trojan horse, to facilitate continued control over the territory by the former imperialists.

It also should be noted that the Westminster model, or any unsubstantially altered version of it, does not address itself to social revolutionary conditions and to the needs for changes in that direction. In the Anglo-Saxon tradition, it tends to leave certain sectors of society, such as the economy, as far as possible outside the area of constitutional arrangements. It also tends to leave outside that area matters related to social or political organization or organizational activity, except insofar as they are concerned with the foundations of formal-legal structure, subversion, treason, etc. Most important, it does not directly address itself to the roots and principal features of the social and political control-structure, such as points of control over the means of production of wealth and the means of distribution of wealth. If anything, it excludes these control points from the formal-legal system, placing them beyond the reach of social-revolutionary elements, as long as these elements can be compelled to play the game by the established rules.

Whatever adjustments are to be made in the future, it is worth noting that the primary motivation on the part of the British rulers in promoting the use of the Westminster model was not social-revolutionary. Formal arrangements for the post-independence regime tended to ignore social differentiations and conflicts. It must be added, however, that the same fundamentals were also ignored by the Nigerian partners in the transfer process, particularly by the northern partners. The combination of an alien origin and the failure to take into account social imbalances and basic social conflicts arising from the transitional processes constitutes a handicap of overwhelming proportions for the Westminster model.

One prime reason for the harmonious transfer of power between

1954 and 1960 was that a group of Nigerians had been trained to accept the system and its implications. Foremost among these were a handful of Nigerians who had become partners—albeit frequently silent ones—in the economy, especially in the economic management of the country, or who had, as officials, been vested with the formal perquisites of power. This produced a certain degree of identity of interests between Europeans and Nigerians, a vested interest that would yield power to outsiders, newcomers, and upstarts only under pressure, never as readily and gracefully as skillful governors-general or colonial secretaries made it appear.

Whether the constitutional-legal structure becomes the focus of a political power struggle will depend in large measure on the concessions made by those who will amend the constitutional documents to placate the social and political forces clamoring for change. Social-revolutionary forces will quite likely tend to ignore the Westminster model whenever possible; but whenever it has value as a social-revolutionary instrumentality—in its adjusted version—they will seek to exploit some of its features for their purposes. Similarly, the status quo forces have recognized in the British model a device for the protection of their interests, for the relative absence of a separation of powers in it more readily permits the welding of basic and superficial power positions for mutual protection and the preservation of the status quo. Feudal institutions and practices, as well as prerogatives acquired under the colonial system, can be subtly introduced or integrated into the institutions and offices of the formal structure without embarrassing publicity and without the impediments usually built into models by the emphasis on stricter separation of executive, legislative, and judicial functions. In general, it is quite doubtful whether any constitutional-legal system—or such subsidiary aspects as parliamentary institutions and practices—can be transferred to any really meaningful degree from one culture to another. Certainly, one should not expect that the 1960 model of the Westminster system can be made operative in that form in the Nigeria of the 1960's. A large number of variables come to mind, all of which tend to impede the operation of a system transferred from one world to another: historic setting, developmental pace, distribution of wealth, value systems, perspectives commonly held, population mobility, degree of public participation in power processes, degree to which consensus mechanism exists, availability of trained and skilled administrators and technicians, communications and transportation, presence of a cohesive actual or potential opposition, religious background, literacy, education, and training.

If some aspects of the British-originated system survive, the following problems will need to be assessed, for the relatively weak separation and balancing features tend to be further weakened by several factors. There is evidence of a tendency to apply indiscriminate political power to nonpolitical aspects of public and private life. Neither the economy, the judicial system, nor the educational system is satisfactorily protected against an arbitrary, massive intrusion of political power. In fact, it may be said that the separation of powers—not practiced as faithfully in more advanced states as one is led to believe—is substantially ineffectual in societies where no really independent forces exist. Those in control of the economy, of the police, and of the armed forces are the effective rulers. They are displaced or influenced primarily by nonconstitutional devices, certainly not by judicial, legislative, or electoral action. Under prevailing conditions—and there is no reason to anticipate significant changes in this respect—the defeat of an individual at the polls does not mean loss of position, income, or prestige as long as he is valuable to the rulers. Similarly, the close connection between public and private finance in a developing country tends to obscure areas of political jurisdiction. Finally, the corruption and control of public funds—which will be major sources of power and influence for some time to come, particularly if welfare-state concepts should predominate in future planning— render such niceties as the separation of powers and the protection of the public domain against irregular incursions from the private side completely inoperative.

Safety Valves for Reform and Change

It is assumed that conditions of political stability require, among other things, adequate provisions in the formal structure for orderly reform and for change, both substantive and procedural. On the surface, the British model used in Nigeria does provide these things; in actuality, however, the system lends itself more to the preservation of the status quo than to change and reform. The predominance of the northern element in the federal government is the result of overvaluation of the quantitative aspect of the universal-franchise feature of British parliamentary democracy, for on the surface, it satisfies the principles of representative government, since more people live in the north than in the south. But at the time the northern group became entrenched at the center, the electoral franchise was practiced in the north under conditions radically different from those assumed to be best for the proper functioning of the constitution. As the system operates, the real rulers, the economically favored and the socially entrenched, remain secure in their positions—as they did in Britain through the centuries. Gradualism becomes the watchword instead of substantive reform and change; constitutional, or formal, changes of government are turned into measures of evading real social progress and reform. Where the relatively inarticulate but real pressures for substantive reform are as great as they are in Nigeria, gradualism as a governing principle becomes a source of instability. It invites revolutionary discontent. Under the Westminster model, which is, according to some, an eminently successful governmental mechanism in Britain, substantive changes are effected only if the public is literate, reasonably educated, and politically participative in large measure. In Nigeria, the public does not yet participate to an appreciable extent in the political processes, aside from the largely mechanical participation in the electoral process. There is as yet no real popular conceptualization of modern government and rule. Under such conditions, the formal system becomes the focus only of peripheral activities, debates over trivia, and relatively insignificant personnel politics at the federal or regional levels, and the substance of politics is left beyond the reach of the people and their representatives.

A country like Nigeria requires substantive social and economic changes to permit its government to meet the contemporary requirements for improved social services, security, and stability. Under those conditions, the formal constitutional system has value only if it lends itself to a full and extensive consideration of these requirements at all levels. Instead, an analysis of parliamentary debates in Nigeria reveals, for instance, that the system obscures and distracts by its preoccupation with peripheral matters; the rules are designed to preserve what is called formality but is, in reality, the status quo. In the more highly developed free societies, substantive changes are brought about by forces operating outside the confines of parliament in open economic competition. And as has been demonstrated elsewhere in the underdeveloped world, the continued frustration of groups dissatisfied with the social and economic order of things results in violent eruptions sooner or later.

The effective channels for reform and change set up under the constitutional system are carefully engineered to permit control over the key strategic points of society, the economy, and the body politic by the rulers legitimized by the departing colonial regime. The coercive powers—the army, the police, and the secret police— are, for a period, being retained in the hands of the colonial power, although barely concealed, to permit the entrenchment of the legitimized successor government. Competition for positions of leadership is restricted and subjected to licensing procedures carefully devised to keep out undesirable candidates. Thus, the social-revolutionary forces are restrained initially from playing significant roles; during the transitional period, they must confine themselves to only an occasional riot or an orderly protest march.

This is not to say that the British model is theoretically *designed* to resist progress and reform. It is to say merely that in Britain, over the years, it seems to have *operated* for just that purpose. Only in this century, under the care of the "mother of parliaments," have real reforms been made possible by real and substantive debates on basic issues. This, however, was not due to formal changes in the constitutional structure; it resulted from changes elsewhere in society, and elsewhere in the world.

In the main, the constitutional structure with which Nigeria was endowed at independence served these purposes: (1) to facilitate the transfer of power to a substantially predetermined elite; (2) to provide sets of principles and guidelines for the formal, mechanical operation of the government along lines favorable to the foreign political and economic interests of both the British and their elite counterparts in Nigeria; (3) to assure, as long as possible, a political balance between the predetermined elite on the one hand and their momentary and potential challengers on the other; and (4) to preserve the status quo in the several regions through the protection of certain groups and through carefully circumscribed and special kinds of individual rights.

It must, of course, be conceded that the British-chaperoned constitutional arrangement strengthened Nigeria politically through the establishment of the very balance that some interpret as a device to divide and rule. There can be no doubt that the federal system itself acts for the time being as a balancing and stabilizing force. For instance, each regional regime is restrained from too wanton an exercise of its powers over ethnic minorities within its boundaries as long as its leaders are compelled to compete with leaders from the other regions for general acceptance and support throughout the country. What is at issue here, however, is the continuing and sustained stability value of that system. It seems that just as the United States' federal system was unable to stave off a physical showdown between fundamentally conflicting social-economic-political forces in the 1860's, so the Nigerian federal system may not be able to prevent such a showdown in the future.

Training Ground for Democracy?

Since World War II, some British colonial experts have held that local government could be a most suitable training ground for democracy in the colonies. They envisaged these specific functions for local government: (1) to provide machinery for the discussion of local needs and for the provision of corresponding services within the competence and capabilities of the local area; (2) to provide machinery for execution at the local level of regional or federal government policy; (3) to provide a consensus mechanism for the resolution of conflicts of interests at the local level; (4) to provide a training ground for political participation and articulation.[3] An important clue to the thinking behind the development of the local government structure was contained in the pronouncement of a colonial secretary: "Only where there is efficient local government acceptable to the people, will it be possible to enforce that degree of community-mindedness and self-discipline among the farmers which is necessary for the proper use of the land and the maintenance of soil fertility."[4]

The emphasis clearly was on training for democracy from the ground up, in the European tradition of town and village councils, and local government was to be the focal point. The future operators of the democratic system were to be trained under the strict supervision and control of the colonial regime, and subsequently under the supervision of African rulers supported by British expatriate administrators. In theory, local government was to become an important safeguard against the exercise of excessive, even dictatorial, powers at the center. It was held that "the organization of essential activities and the control of essential services on a local basis by the people of a community is one of the strengths of the British system, as it can be of African systems also."[5]

However, there are a number of problems concerning the operation of local government in a setting that is essentially tribal and traditional. Parochialism, intensely developed as a result of the pronounced insular tendencies of African tribes, actually is further encouraged by the development of local government as conceived by Secretary Griffith. The narrow view is given legitimacy and significance in the political context, and it is raised to the level of an inherent right. Inevitably, once the power hierarchy is under the sway of tribal authority, or identified with it, traditional concepts of social organization and development soon engulf the modern political system, become dominant, and then become institutionalized. Reaction becomes entrenched, and local government becomes a rallying point for the status quo forces. Its major function then is to assure the preservation of bases for reaction to modernization and for combat against the secular forces in society.

Another set of problems affecting the stability value of local government arises from the conflict between the multiplicity of interests at the local level and those, for instance, at the higher regional level. Since the territorial and functional division of power is one purpose of local government, the focus of politics is likely to be at cross-purposes among different, even if adjacent, areas. In more advanced societies, this does not present an insurmountable hurdle to good government, but in the absence of a well-developed consensus mechanism, such diffusive tendencies are likely to be more of a hindrance. Stresses and strains are introduced into the policy-making machinery at the next higher level that may outweigh, in social value, any advantages in the spheres of political training potentially derived from local government. There is very little evidence in the pronouncements by spokesmen of either the colonial regime or the Nigerian successor regime of an adequate realization of these difficulties. The suspicion that diversification of the power hierarchies in a country as diffuse ethnically, culturally, and linguistically as Nigeria, serves the specific political purposes of colonial interests cannot entirely be discounted. This is not to say that motivations of this kind uniformly dominated British thinking on the subject; it is to say that the absence of critical discussions about the real operational problems of local government under these conditions reflects unfavorably upon the promoters of the system. It reflects, at best, a preoccupation with values of low priority at a time when fundamental social and political changes need to be engineered, a lack of realization of the need for developmental speed, and a failure to appreciate the fundamental difference between the British experience at home and the requirements of twentieth-century Nigeria.

Under post-independence conditions, local government is subjected to additional pressures and shocks. Both the removal of expatriate officials—or, at least, the reduction of their power and influence—and the sharply increasing demands for services have left budding local-government units with an acute shortage of qualified personnel, funds, and equipment to cope with the most essential public needs. This increases the dependence of local units upon higher levels, and it brings down to the local level strangers and even traditional enemies. In addition, there are the tendencies of nationalist politicians to object to any structural arrangements that tend to retard progress—as viewed by them, of course—and to become impatient with the relatively slow processes of local government and administration. Under such conditions, friction develops, which does not enhance stability. Because the ways of local government are apt to be inadequate during periods of rapid social and technological development, officials and political leaders at higher levels frequently prefer to disregard local government. Frequently, while some local officials are going through the motions of administering a directive, other, countervailing directives are being dispatched from higher headquarters. An excessive interference with the operations of local government need not be a product only of dictatorial pressure; it can also result from the impatience of those who deem themselves more representative of the people than the local leaders.

As a matter of fact, the precedent for disregarding local government, whether traditional or modern, was set by the colonial rulers who administered all colonies through parallel organizations or systems. The system of "indirect rule" was never as indirect as is commonly represented; it was indirect only as long as the traditional authority accepted the dictate of the colonial regime.* Wherever the need for such interference arose, in conjunction with a road project or a mining operation, for instance, the colonial regime wasted little time before it reached past traditional authority to assure the execution of its own policies, and, of course, it dealt summarily with recalcitrants among the traditional leaders. Similarly, the modern African rulers are not inclined to be patient and considerate with what they deem are vital interests. The slow and ponderous processes of tradition-minded local-government units, with their indeterminate "palavers," are not acceptable to the modern leaders-in-a-hurry. Problems of mass education, massive population transfers, and gigantic (by traditional standards) construction projects are well beyond the ken of most district and municipal councils and their administrative personnel.[6] The problems of fiscal and resource management, the coordination of local needs—primitive and unimportant if measured against regional or federal development needs—with high-level planning and projection, all are beyond local capabilities, conceptually, politically, and technically. Secretary Griffith's reference to "efficiency" in modern local government appears to be misplaced.

Another source of difficulties stems from the temptation to tamper with the local-government structure for social or political revolutionary purposes. Frequently, structure will be adapted to the regional and party political goals. Where possible, it will be employed to perform political rather than administrative or educational and training functions. An outstanding example was the provincial councils introduced in the Eastern Region in 1959. They clearly were the political tools of the regional government; there were signs that the other regions had no different intentions concerning their versions of the provincial councils.

In terms of personnel attitudes, local government in Nigeria,

* Indirect rule was based on the use of traditional native authority as agencies of colonial rule.

particularly in the southern sections, will suffer for some time to come from the instability incurred by what has been described as the "upward draft" in underdeveloped countries. It focuses the attention of lower-rank civil servants and local-government officers otherwise classified upon the higher and highest offices. Until the top ranks in the political and administrative hierarchies are more adequately staffed and qualified reserves build up in competition for each position, lower-rank officials will be disinclined to live out their careers in the bush. Local-government posts, under such conditions, are, for many, at best merely way-stations on the way to something better. The implications of this in terms of the political power and influence of political leaders should be clear.

The New and the Old

As has been dramatically demonstrated in Ghana and Guinea, where power is absolutely in the hands of secular regimes, traditional rule has no effective defenses left. Local government is too thoroughly integrated into the centrally directed and controlled political machine to lend itself, for long, to manipulation by local traditional rulers. Similarly, in the Eastern Region of Nigeria, to a greater extent, and in the Western Region, to a somewhat lesser extent, traditional rulers lack independent powers to resist pressures from the regional level or to influence local-government units in contravention of regional policies. Consequently, although stabilizing influences may be emanating from traditional rulers, the latter find no sympathetic locus of power, no real opportunity to be effective, unless they are invited to perform some minor functions for the modern regimes in return for services rendered. In spite of appearances, the traditional rulers in the west, the *obas*, for example, have long ago been sucked into the vortex of secular politics. Their courts are hotbeds of pressure and interest-group activities—as has been the case, no doubt, since the inception of the system. What is novel about current conditions is that the traditional rulers have become objects in the power struggle: They are used. The regional government is the sole source of meaningful legitimacy, for it can endow a chief with prestige and influence or assure his ruin. Only if the traditional ruler, or the supporters and interest groups clustered around him, manages to gamble successfully in the partisan political power struggle within the region can he hope to retain a vestige of independence. Whenever or wherever a traditional ruler in the Western Region challenges the regional government and the dominant party there, he does so because he enjoys the support of an opposing political party, possibly from another region.

In the north, all power is vested in the hands of the Islamic rulers, and local government is totally integrated into the traditional structure. In maintaining law and order, the prevailing system draws on traditional authority to be effective because traditional government *is* local government there. Under those circumstances, the system might be allocated a rather high stability value; for it has demonstrated, on several occasions, an ability to suppress, or at least to control, oppositional activities, including those legalized under federal or regional statutes and regulations. Whether it will be equally effective in controlling social-revolutionary movements is questionable. There are as yet relatively few safety valves, few areas of accommodation of oppositional forces in the north. Severe revolutionary shocks may be long in coming, but they are building up, both inside and outside the region. Under conditions prevailing throughout Africa, too close an identification of the secular with the spiritual-traditional —in this case, feudal—regime must, in the long run, prove to be a major unstabilizing factor.[7]

A Losing Proposition

Cowan notes that the British colonial administration met the changing needs of local government in the southern parts "in the same way that had been evolved to meet an analogous situation at home fifty years previously." [8] That is to say that expression was given to the interests of the rapidly developing middle class, which insisted on being represented in government at least at the local level. The question might be asked whether or not, under existing conditions, these interests, recognized by the British, actually play a significant part in politics? In Britain, the same elements that tended to control local government during its period of growth also dominated the national level. In Nigeria, local government, wherever conditions favored such participation, served as an outlet for the African middle class commercial and professional interests, but colonial rule prevailed at the top. Following independence, the locus of African political activity shifted to the regional and federal levels, and what may at one time have superficially resembled early British county and city government quickly assumed an entirely different appearance. As a result of the nationalist tide, the new elite did not grow from local-government roots or from local clusters of social power. It poured into positions of power at the top, through openings provided by the colonial power, and bypassed not only the legitimized but localized African middle-class and professional groupings, but also the traditional rulers, who had been tied to the local structure. Under the circumstances, the introduction of a representative government of sorts, more or less a feature of British administration everywhere, cannot be evaluated as a stabilizing factor in the emergent society. The elements to be appeased through participation in the political process—that is, those with substantial political bargaining power—are not those trained in representative government at the local level, but those trained elsewhere. Thus, in terms of significant political performance in post-independence Nigeria, the introduction of representative-government practices at the local level cannot be considered analogous to the British experience. The shift of the point of gravity of political action was too sudden, the swing from one extreme to another too wide, to permit the gradual adaptation of local government to the exigencies of regional and federal politics.

Cowan observes that the councils may still gain a substantial measure of popular respect if they manage to keep pace with "the slowly growing demands for new local services in the country districts." [9] There is every reason to believe that this possibility exists; even in a system like the Soviet system, local government has attained a measure of utility and respect, in spite of the over-powering pressures from the central planning agencies and from the political bosses. However, as a factor in the stability-producing processes in Nigeria, local government is not likely to assume too important a role in the foreseeable future. The power struggle at the regional level, and at the federal level as well, centers on economic and social issues too sharply divergent from those at the local level—especially while local governments are advancing from earlier stages of infancy. Any shift at the federal level that involves a change from the northern-dominated to a southern-dominated coalition is bound to bring in its wake a massive shift of public opinion and, consequently, massive changes in the representation patterns. It will be relatively easy for a new group at the federal center to excite the imagination of people concerning local-government services—a situation quite unlike that prevailing, for example, in nineteenth-century Britain. Already, bids for loyalties have been extended from the regional level downward, and they offer as bait promises to provide modern services. Unlike their counterparts in earlier Britain, Nigerians in the southern sections, especially, are taught by tutors—and agitators—from all over the world to be dissatisfied with present conditions. And inasmuch as the improvements promised are so far beyond the capabilities of most local-government councils, whether economically, technically, or conceptually, it is unlikely that the voting public will see permanent value in local-government institutions. More likely, since order must be maintained, they can be calmed down only by rigorous nondemocratic control of their social and technological appetites.

A key problem affecting the over-all social and political utility of local government derives, of course, from the availability and adequacy of local funds for local purposes. Since the pressures building up in Nigeria favor rapid social and technological progress on a wide scale, local government will for some time to come be inadequately financed. The Colonial Office conference on local government in 1951 noted that in order for local-government authorities to work efficiently toward developing a civic sense and governmental initiative at the local level, they must "be given financial responsibility and have adequate funds at their disposal upon which to exercise it." The report then noted that "in few local-government areas are the funds which can be raised locally sufficient to provide the works and services demanded by modern ideas of the duties of states toward the individual citizen, and in some areas the funds available at present are inadequate to provide even the minimum acceptable standards of, for instance, *elementary* education." [10] There is no reason to believe that this problem has been materially resolved since 1951 or that it can be met adequately in the foreseeable future. Modern ideas of the duties of the state toward the individual are radically different from those that prevailed when local government came of age in Britain. Concepts of social welfare, for instance, now receiving their impetus from "conditions of peaceful coexistence," are likely to be even more radical.

Thus, local government in Nigeria will have to overcome major obstacles to gain a sufficient measure of popular respect to permit it to meet the requirements of the age. Organizationally and conceptually, local government moves between the Scylla of traditional rule and the Charybdis of modern secular rule at the regional levels. As local government manages to develop standard operating procedures, rules of conduct, concepts of organization and operation, and accumulates the personnel required, frequent and often radical changes will be decreed by the commanding regional authorities. As a result, local government frequently lapses into a state of suspended animation until the new concepts and rules have filtered down, pursuant to initial directives. Then, while the new procedures are being understood, coordinated, interpreted, adapted, and translated into local policy and action, the grass grows back on the village streets. There are signs that traditional concepts and practices are infiltrating the local-government machinery as a result of popular disenchantment with the local consequences of the new age.

Regional politics also suck local governments into political battles substantially unrelated to the interests of their communities. Many local units in all regions of Nigeria are, in fact, political battlefields for regional forces. Where the stakes demand it, local units are subjected to pressures that prevent them from settling down to the business for which they were created and compel local authorities to spend their time trying to outguess the powers at the center. Because of the likelihood of administrative error under the conditions prevailing in Nigeria, nearly all local-government agencies are vulnerable, and any superior political force intent on discrediting a given local authority has little difficulty in finding ample legal grounds to persecute it to the point of submission.

Part Two

ANATOMY OF THE POLITICAL GAME

3

Values and Ideas

The Birth of an Idea System: Perspectives

While it is, of course, most difficult to develop universally valid theories concerning the relationship between perspectives and political stability, it may nevertheless be fruitful to treat the matter speculatively. Lasswell's definition may be useful here: "A perspective is a pattern of identifications, demands, and expectations." [1] For present purposes, two categories of perspective patterns with special relevance to political stability are discussed: those of the elite, or elite groups, and those of the masses as reflected by institutionalized and other less formal, spontaneous opinion-forming agencies.

Since Nigerian society is subjected to communication pressures on a broad front and from a variety of directions, it is extremely unlikely that perspective patterns of reasonably lasting validity will be formed for some time to come. For these reasons and for others, more specific and technical opinion research remains in the embryonic stage. As everywhere else, communications are being revolutionized. Neither education nor training in literacy and technical skills, essential in perspective formation, is sufficiently stabilized in scope and method to permit reliable estimates as to the results obtained or obtainable. Under conditions as fluid as those in Nigeria, basic concepts of social organization, functions, or role performance, and expectations, identifications, or demands should be treated as unknown factors in a general appraisal of stability in the country.

Fundamental values, ideas, and perspectives can attain a reasonable degree of permanence in some areas of human activity less exposed to changing influences. Thus, in many "corners" of the country, expectations about the functions and purposes of govern-ment—commonly, traditional rule—are relatively constant and measurable. Likewise, in sectors of the culture where opinion-forming or influencing agencies are relatively highly developed and skilled enough to make an impact and are operating in con-centrated fashion, a degree of constancy may be attained. In the Northern Region, nearly all opinion-forming agencies are integral parts of the political and social control structure; hence, perspec-tive patterns are most likely those deemed desirable by the rulers and in accord with their precepts. In the southern sections, on the other hand, where the all-encompassing and controlling force of Islam is not dominant, secular agencies and forces must be em-ployed to influence perspective formation. Hence, part of the political struggle there addresses itself to control over the media of opinion-formation—newspapers, radio, and television—and to contact work with local opinion-makers or leaders.

Lasswell points to additional considerations regarding the value of perspectives in the stability equation: "The stability of a rule varies with the intensity of perspectives (of both elite and mass) sustaining the elite."[2] Intensity of perspectives here means the intensity of adherence to the prevailing or predominant ideology. It also means "passionate" belief and conviction.

One basic defect in the rule-perspective relationship in the Ni-gerian case derives, most likely, from the absence of a universally acceptable and understood rationale for the existence and func-tioning of the state called Nigeria. Although at the outset of its independent existence Nigeria appeared to be more viable than most other states emerging on the continent at the time, it still is not to be compared with European states of similar size and popu-lation. There is no substantial Nigerian tradition of nationalist pressure toward existence as a nationally and ethnically independ-ent state. The stimulant for militant efforts such as insurrection, the call for "liberation," has been absent, and any efforts at an artificial creation of a national mythology, a Nigerian ideology, will be unproductive because of the overwhelming forces arraigned against it from the side of tribalism, religious juxta-positions, regional diversities, and cultural chasms. Under such circumstances, stability becomes problematic if it is dependent upon intense, passionate adherence to, let us say, Nigerian nation-alist ideology. Neither the masses nor the elite can be expected, under these conditions, to develop the kind of perspectives—dura-ble, constant, and in depth—requiring and bringing forth sacrifices, intense devotion and loyalty, discipline, dedication, and faith.

Since the environment is extremely fluid and the centrifugal (state-destroying) forces are perhaps more substantial here than elsewhere on the continent, the chances that these difficulties will be resolved in favor of nationally useful perspectives during a period of quiet construction are extremely slim. The elite groups will find it increasingly difficult to isolate the masses from the outside world, as their European predecessors did during forma-tive periods there. Thus, the weaknesses in the Nigerian situation are likely to become more accentuated. "Insurrection of thought" is, therefore, an ever-present threat because the thought complex that treats Nigeria as a generally acceptable framework for social and political action is neither formulated nor established, and the conditions are not conducive to its development toward a pre-dominant and unifying political idea system. In other words, one problem for the leaders is to formulate an idea system, an ide-ology, based on the Nigerian nation-state concept, which offers significant value not only to themselves but to substantial seg-ments of the population as well. What is required are patterns of political conceptualization and corresponding doctrines to sustain the elite, render it cohesive and sufficiently single-minded to rule, and to sustain its elite positions. The effort should prove to be as difficult for some time to come as trying to construct a house on shifting sands.

Additional problems arise over the absence of intellectual depth. There is nothing permanent about this particular problem, nor should it be understood that there are in Nigeria no persons who command the intellectual depth required for socially valid perspective formation. It is the general scarcity of such persons and the shallowness of intellectual conceptualization and attachments that create the problem; for socially valid perspectives are those that are capable of generating sustained individual or group action or practices rather than erratic, isolated, atomized, and individually unique responses. Too many counterstimulants are being introduced from too many sources to permit the growth of perspective patterns in the minds of Nigerians who barely possess a rudimentary knowledge of the alien idea system introduced into the area by the colonial power.[3]

Frequently articulated and widely held concepts are as yet not held firmly enough, not sufficiently understood, assimilated, and personalized, to withstand the stresses and strains of political and cultural transition. Even entirely erroneous or misunderstood concepts, relationships, and ideas are politically more significant than concepts not at all comprehended, digested, or assimilated. In Nigeria, for some time to come, the number of persons in elite positions, as well as in society generally, who are capable of comprehending socially significant data and relationships, making social perspectives part of their personality structure, even for only a short time, and translating them into acts or practices, sustained demands or expectations, is going to be rather limited. If perspectives *appear* to be rather strong, and intensely adhered to by either mass or elite elements, one may be in the presence only of a passing phenomenon, for the idea structure may suddenly collapse and evaporate without leaving significant traces for historians to ponder. Thus, expectations related to the attainment of political independence, the elite-mass relationship centering on that event, and its immediate consequences may have evaporated almost as soon as the event took place.

Nigerian nationalism, democracy, socialism, Christianity, etc., none of which is rooted in tradition or significantly related to the predominant traditional culture patterns, may be encountered in superficially conducted opinion surveys or in what appear to be reflections of sustained public opinion. But, in reality, they are spontaneous mass psychological products. Even fairly articulate responses to questions related to these concepts or idea systems may be encountered in interviews with Nigerians in all walks of life. Yet none may be comprehended, none has really become part of the perception system, and, probably, none has been assimilated to the personality. All may readily be swept away by counterstimulants, especially when such are couched in terms more closely related to the social environment of the individuals concerned. In the Northern Region, especially where Islam is entrenched, the predominant political idea system, identified as it is with the predominant culture system, has had the historic opportunity to entrench itself in the minds of the elite and the masses. In the case of the masses, one does, of course, deal with a vernacularization of the system; but in substantial sections of the north, everything operates in favor of perception in depth of the predominant idea system toward the creation of political stability simply because the intensity of perspectives sustaining the elite is assured.

How relevant to this discussion are the traditional ways, the tribal value system, outside the area of predominance of Islam? Anthropologists like Professor Melville J. Herskowits attach a high value to the role of traditional institutions—and presumably also of tradition-connected social and political perspectives—in the transition period. To accept this, one would have to assume both legitimacy and utility value in the modern setting for the traditional ways, institutions, and practices. Although it may be valid to hold that ideal conditions should include, among other things, the temporary extension of tribal values until transition has passed the dangerous periods, ideals of that kind have little merit in terms of elite or mass psychology. In practice, traditional values survive in other than purely symbolic forms only where modernity is barred from massive intrusion, and the zones in which this applies are rapidly shrinking. In places where institutions like chieftaincy survive only for symbolic purposes, occasionally only for sentimental ones, the point of no return has been passed. Traditional ways, of course, keep their hold on the minds of the people. They may be equivalent in many respects to equally tenuous, doubt-ridden idea systems now introduced from outside, but they no longer have the sustaining power to be assessed highly as a stability-producing force. Modern ways, in practical, significant respects, are not likely to be related to traditional ways. As far as utility in the modern setting is concerned, the inability of traditional systems to develop ideological or technical skills to cope with the social, political, and psychological problems of this century becomes more evident every day. It is unlikely, therefore, that deep-seated, reasonably lasting perspectives and values will emerge from the traditional system with political stability value in the post-independence state. The great issues confronting a nation such as Nigeria are related to the experiences under tribal systems only in a literary sense. The individual psychologically leaves the tribal setting long before he departs physically; he becomes part of modernity long before he sheds the vestiges of traditional existence. This is becoming obvious in even the remotest areas.

Area of Agreement?

Is there a consensus mechanism in Nigeria sufficiently well-developed to facilitate the discussion and determination of ideological or issue propositions, especially propositions of relevance to the stability of the state? Frequently, the pre-independence stages are mistaken for ideological germinating periods. It is evident, of course, that "anticolonialism," "Africanism," "nationalism," and related pre-independence stimuli create the prerequisites for the growth of ideological movements. Movements thus created, however, have little value for the post-independence state when competing elites and claimants for positions of power, now stripped of the common but superficial ideological garment or symbolism, are on their own. Then the realistic problems of nationhood present themselves for substantive discussion and for action. Nigeria did not produce a predominant national ideology, or even a predominant regional ideology, at the time of independence—excepting, of course, Islam, which is rather restricted in its utility as a consensus mechanism under modern conditions.

Under the colonial regime, the consensus mechanism within which ideological discussions, if any, were conducted was primarily that provided by the colonial administration. The significant participants were only the culturally and politically assimilated Africans, and of course the Europeans themselves. The principal forums were government offices, certain exclusive clubs, some courts, and some schools. For the African counterelite—those aspiring to replace the European rule—there was a large variety of meeting places, but they lacked a steady, active, and reasonably well-informed clientele. On the European side, however, ideological discussions were exceedingly limited in scope and of little intellectual value; the personnel who were participating most prominently in the important opinion-directing functions were predominantly civil servants, commercial employees and managers, and a few missionaries. Most important, the intellectual ability of most of the leaders was too marginal to permit them to evolve meaningful generalizations about Africa, Nigeria, or models and methods of social organization, action, and beliefs. Ideologically, the centers of colonial rule were, essentially, void of intellectual stimulation. Pre-independence was a period of ideological poverty and starvation.

The only medium that made a limited attempt at formulation and articulation of significant social and political generalizations was the press. Lead articles by a brilliant young Nigerian were outstanding until he decided to move into the politically less sensitive field of foreign policy—that is, the foreign policy of other countries. But even the staunchly Africanist *West African Pilot* now and then departed from the pattern of undisciplined partisan pamphleteering to produce a piece of insight and value. But attempts by Nigerian leaders were puny and ineffectual: They had not yet developed a conceptual framework for ideological development. Not even Dr. Azikiwe, representing the best Nigeria had produced in the way of an articulator of political thought and philosophy, had settled on a meaningful theme for the political development of Nigeria after the granting of independence. Consequently, his party, the National Congress of Nigeria and the Cameroons (NCNC), was ideologically disoriented; its exclusive focus during the critical years of growth and maturation was the personality of the leader.* The same can be said, essentially, of the Action Group, the creation of another brilliant Nigerian, Chief Obafemi Awolowo. Much of what might have appeared to be an ideological exercise represented a thoughtless display of borrowed goods, alien in origin, politically and socially indigestible. Thus, Nigeria, at the time of independence, had developed neither the form nor the substance of a consensus mechanism to permit the development, in turn, of perspectives of direct relevance to the organization, functioning, and survival of the modern state.

Cornerstones of an Idea System

Social goals are not yet sufficiently delineated to play a role in the formulation of attitudes or perspectives of material bearing on the problem under investigation. To discover trends or directions within which answers may be obtained, one would have to find workable answers to such questions as these: What are the social goals of the "revolution of rising expectations"? What kind of living standards are desired? What kind of living standards are desired by the rulers for themselves and for the masses and, in turn, by the masses for themselves and for the rulers? In realistic terms, are the rulers and the masses addressing themselves to the reproduction of Western, Eastern-Communist, or other models? To what extent does the United States model actually enter into the discussion? What images arise when the people of Nigeria address themselves to their own future?

Partly as a result of economic instability and uncertainty, of

* In 1962, the NCNC changed its name to the National Council of Nigerian Citizens.

the absence of long-range perspectives and value attachments, the will to make sacrifices to gain long-range advantages and social or political national values has, as yet, not developed sufficiently. Neither the leaders, with few exceptions, nor the masses show signs of the courage required to attain broad national goals by mass discipline. Few of the Nigerian leaders are prepared to provide the necessary leadership to guide their people, even if only on the regional level, toward the social, economic, and political goals that are practical and realizable. Instead, too many leaders tend to loosen what discipline there has been in the tribal setting through promises that blandly ignore the means by which they can be realized. This raises a very fundamental question: Can democracy develop the discipline required for the forced economic and social marches to which the people of this or any other under-developed country may have to be subjected before the promised goals can be brought into view?

For the new elite at the time of independence, Nigeria primarily represented not a society in which one believed "with passionate conviction," but one which was more of a vehicle for personal advancement. For the masses, it was a source of miraculous benefits; for the traditional rulers and their supporters, it represented social-revolutionary forces to be resisted and, if possible, destroyed —or, at least, subverted to forms more in keeping with traditional thoughts and practices. The elite's attachment to the emergent society was transitory. There were few signs that a more positive, more pronounced, and more durable attachment would develop in the immediate post-independence years. The devotion to the new Nigerian society was no more passionate than the personal commitment to law offices, hospitals, medical offices, laboratories, schools, or secretarial services. Business, professional, and even governmental positions and offices reflected an air of transience. One seemed to be waiting for something else, something better. Society had not yet crystallized to the point where individuals and groups could locate themselves with regard to society and their proven abilities and worth. Competence could not be measured to the individual's satisfaction; and because the authority to set standards had as yet not been established to the individual's satisfaction, the individual was not yet prepared to accept the fiat of what at best was a growing society.

The categories of restraints operating in, let us say, a North American advanced society against dishonesty, promiscuity, and venality in government are extremely weak in Nigeria—especially in the cases of individuals and groups who have become separated from their traditional environment and are not yet attached to an alternate setting. Under these and similarly conditioned situations of individual and group mobility, stability of character, of value judgment, and of perspectives have not yet become integral parts of societal patterns. Personal responsibility toward one's fellow men still lacks a clearly recognizable focus. The fraud, the mountebank, the cheat, and the fixer do not yet have to face up to a critical public, for public opinion has not yet crystallized to act as a restraint.[4] Moreover, in a society where living standards are exceedingly low and where opportunities for private employment are few, rewards far outdistance risks for those who find it convenient to flaunt traditional or—where such have been partially developed—modern concepts of morality or legality.[5] Restraints built into the traditional patterns of behavior do not operate effectively where traditional rule has lost authority, where the traditional system is disintegrating, where the social and spiritual reference points, the "personality anchors," have disappeared in a mass of as yet unrecognizable new reference points. The secular restraint apparatus—that is, legal and political authority, as well as economic sanctions—have as yet not materialized to the point where sufficiently aggressive individuals or groups may be convinced that the risks of defiance of the legal order, for instance, outweigh the benefits derived from illegality or generally improper conduct. The system of rewards and punishments in a society such as this is not yet developed to the point where the individual or the group intent on defiance or deviation from the generally accepted norm, if any, can readily gauge his personal or group conduct by reference to known standards. Under these circumstances, one cannot speak of restraints against sudden and massive shifts in value judgment.

Many social values are derived from, or sustained by, reference to sources of legitimacy. In the state of transition in which Nigeria will remain for some time to come, established sources rapidly become obsolescent because they become alien and remote; but where such sources are derived from the newly independent African regime, they are vulnerable because they are novel, untested, artificial, incipient, and unrelated to the real power structure.

Formally, Nigeria set out on its path of national existence as a Western-style democracy. This implies the accentuation of the individual, his rights, and his interests. Yet Nigerian society may not be able to afford the luxury of individualism or the protection of individual interests or rights. The problem is perhaps best dramatized by the fact that in 1956 35 million Nigerians were cared for medically by 600 registered medical practitioners, 75 of whom were foreigners licensed to practice locally under special conditions. Since it is estimated that in some parts of the country only 50 per cent of the children attain the age of five, that there are nearly 500,000 lepers, and that in the Northern Region alone there are probably more than 200,000 blind persons, the shortage of medical personnel spells overwhelming difficulties for Western-style democracy in Nigeria. What are the choices open to a surgeon who recognizes the overwhelming demand for his services and also the overwhelming need for the preservation of the life of, let us say, the region's only irrigation specialist or expert on banking? Should the policy guiding this and similar vital services be "first come, first served," or should it be elitist, discriminatory? What rights has the illiterate farmer who walked fifteen miles to stand all night at the hospital gates in order to be the first served in the morning? How do his rights compare with those of the emir, the chief, the political leader—not by monetary standards alone, but by the standards of a society confronted by overpowering social needs? Does the country's youth have the right, guaranteed under the rules of Western democracy, to make individual career choices, or should, and will, the value of a young man's life be assessed in terms of the developing society's interest?

It should be clear without further argument that the political stability of Nigeria requires steady technological advance. Although the British made substantial contributions to the creation of a corps of skilled Nigerian technicians, the major body of scientists and technicians, especially in the most essential services and functions, will for some time be aliens. What will be the impact of their foreign origin on their effectiveness and, more directly, on technological progress? How will their national origin and their alien status affect their role performance as initiators, bearers, and agents of new and, most likely, socially revolutionary techniques? Will science be generally accepted under these circumstances, and will its disciples be permitted to range freely? It seems that in a relatively open society appeals of a parochial type directed against foreign influences would be invited where social-revolutionary measures are either recommended or actually taken by foreigners. This has as yet not been put to the test in Nigeria to any significant extent. In the north, where the problem assumes severest proportions, technological change has been critically retarded; in the southern areas, technological progress has been achieved gradually and in close liaison with indigenous forces and practices. The problem is likely to become acute when more incisive improvements are undertaken with greater shock effect on indigenous society and without the diplomatic, and often quite skillful, control exercised previously by the British.

Lipset holds that the "stability of any given democracy depends not only on economic development but also on the effectiveness and the legitimacy of its political system." [6] To him, "legitimacy" involves the capacity of the system to engender and maintain the belief that the existing political institutions are the most appropriate ones for the society. According to this view, stability may be threatened by a crisis of legitimacy occurring during the transition to a new social structure under certain conditions that include status changes of major conservative institutions and exclude major political groups from access to the system. In Nigeria, the British institution of monarchy, one of the residues of the colonial regime, represents one important transitional device to cushion the shock attending the transfer of formal power. Likewise, the crisis is postponed or blurred in outline by those elements in the traditional structure that have become identified with the new regime—the legitimized traditional rulers. Legitimacy here was either derived from colonial authority and accepted by the new secular rulers or was conferred by the Nigerian successor government.

In spite of shock-reduction techniques, as power is transferred from colonial to indigenous control, some groups are left out of the allocation and distribution of positions and instrumentalities of power, income, and prestige. Among others are the extremist and fringe elements in the nationalist movements (the Zikists, Dr. Azikiwe's angry young men, come to mind) and the Nigerian equivalents of the groups of die-hards surrounding European dictators during the periods of struggle for power—groups that, in all instances, seem to be soon subjected to severe control, if not persecution, once power has been attained. Other passed-over groups are found among the middle-level administrators, even among the top-level ones, in some instances; among the clerks and white-collar employees in commerce, industry, and government-operated enterprises; and among the professionals and the intelligentsia generally. The latter, together with the African leaders of the embryonic trade-union movement, represents perhaps the most potent challenge to the legitimacy of the British-installed regime. Indirectly traceable to the attainment of independence is the deterioration in the relative power position of the traditional leaders and those elements of society whose influence depended primarily or heavily upon certain modes of production. Basically, Lipset observes, "the survival of the new political democracies of Asia and Africa will depend on their ability to meet the needs of their populations over a prolonged period, which will probably mean their ability to cope with industrialization."[7] It is unlikely that democratic institutions and practices will have a great functional value to those who have a vested interest in the strengthening and the continued stability of the newly established Nigerian state. But even if there should be a missionary, idealistic attachment to democratic ways among the ruling elite, it is unlikely that democratic ways will materially assist Nigeria to achieve a steady rate of industrialization commensurate with economic and political requirements. If minimum goals either on a regional or on a national basis are not attained, then the claims to legitimacy by proponents of democratic ways will be subjected to counterclaims by what may appear to be more efficient managers of material and manpower resources. In all likelihood, democratic ways are deemed legitimate only by those whose positions were attained by the processes operating under the colonial version of the British model and by those who, preparatory to the introduction of nondemocratic ways, find democratic procedures convenient avenues to power.

4

Effective and Ineffective Rulers

Sources of Leadership

Political stability depends, of course, on socio-economic environmental factors and circumstances. But given substantially similar environmental settings, the variations in such matters as the political behavior, perspectives, and inner-organizational strength of the policy- and decision-makers (the principal control group, the elite, and the ruling elements) may prove to be the determinants of the stability of the system. For present purposes, only those aspects of the personnel factor in the political process are evaluated that are deemed critical to the operation of essential aspects of the system, especially with regard to political stability. Disregarded are the historical and anthropological data that have only limited relevance to the modern political system. This decision is governed by the assumption that not every leader is of consequence to the modern political processes and that only a few key functional areas in the country—and there only a few key sectors—are of sufficient import to be classified as critical. Major determinants are the opportunities for access to the sources of political power as defined earlier, to the effective control structure, to major channels of communication, to prestige-producing factors, and to the key administrative and service positions.

Leaders do not by their own efforts attain positions of power and influence; key people are not placed solely by their own efforts. What are the sources of power and influence in the contemporary Nigerian setting? Because of the exercise of total political power by the colonial regime prior to independence, few if any sources of power and influence existed outside the sphere of colonial control. This included the traditional system or systems. The ruling elite was made up entirely of social, economic, political, and administrative extensions of European power and influence. The strictest controls were exercised over the subleadership group and over existing and potential sources of a counter, anticolonial elite. The controls of elite recruitment were exclusively in the hands of the Europeans. If democratic procedures were employed in the pre-independence structure, they applied primarily to the bearers or principal expatriate beneficiaries of colonial power. The introduction of self-government modified the autocratic pattern of colonial rule, but it should be noted that the period of self-government was not extended enough to serve as a training or development period. At any rate, even during the self-government stages, colonial rule jealously guarded the key control points in the system: the economy, administration, police, and armed forces.

Thus, under carefully controlled conditions, what may be called a "foster elite" is produced by the colonial regime. In many respects, it represents products of the culture-transplantation processes, for which the British have become renowned. At first, the new rulers are established in subordinate positions, as understudies. Designated by the Colonial Office and its representatives in the colonial territories, they are introduced through the administrative, educational, business, or industrial systems. They may be judges, lawyers, teachers, businessmen, clerks, or managers; they may also be accepted leaders in the traditional system. They are well-read, ideologically-culturally related to the home country, but astonishingly unfamiliar with the social and political setting within which they are to function. Being so thoroughly European-oriented, they have a vested interest in the maintenance of closest ties with the "home country." They are committed to the maintenance of at least fundamental aspects of the colonial system and, if given the choice, to the law and order it seeks to uphold. Their claim to "indigenous" status should not be accepted without further assessment; they may, in fact, be more European than African. But proximity to the primary sources of power and influence serves to transfer upon themselves at least some key attributes of rule.

There is a suspicion, expressed by numerous nationalists among the Nigerians, that the colonial regime deliberately fostered the growth of the Senior Service not only to meet the requirements of public administration, but to leave behind a kind of Trojan horse. Of interest in that connection are the findings and recommendations of the so-called Harragin Commission which, in 1946, reviewed certain aspects of the public service. The Commission foresaw the creation of an upper class of executives, of "people who could make decisions and carry on managerial functions." The need for such an artificial class was believed to be urgent because "the Nigerian society [was] an amorphous one, in which there was nothing like an upper class, middle class, and the proletariat." The Commission felt that an upper class was the *sine qua non* of political stability. On at least one occasion, it was suggested by a Nigerian that in order to secure the "foster elite," the colonial regime developed a highly unbalanced salary structure which left the Senior Service far above the rest as a special interest group.[1]

Outstanding among other significant power and influence-producing sources are the sources derived from the traditional-feudal structure in the north and the economic sources derived from the participation of Africans in the commercial and trading activities in the southern section. In the north, with the exception of some cities, identification with the traditional ruling element, regardless of personal qualification, is a fundamental prerequisite for securing admission to elite status. The withdrawal of favor by an emir or another bearer of royal authority is tantamount to political oblivion. Even the accumulation of economic wealth alone is not adequate to challenge the power of traditional rulers and their representatives in the legal structure, if such an accumulation independent of traditional rule is at all possible.

In the southern section, traditional status matters only in a relatively few instances. The struggle for power is far more open and competitive, and factors other than status are required to produce influence and power. The traditional rulers, such as the *obas* in the Western Region, are still powerful, but they find it more and more expedient to supplement traditional sources of power with secular, modern sources as well. Moreover, they find it progressively more difficult to pass their power and prestige on to others by mere association or invocation of tribal selection machinery. If traditional rulers, or other tribal claimants to positions of power, wish to acquire political prestige of their own in the contemporary setting, they must become identified and associated with the new secular rulers, or else acquire independent economic means.

As for economic sources of power and influence alone—that is, without political office or the aid of traditional prestige—a pattern is developing in which everyone who has the opportunity to do so acquires some sources of income by tapping the rapidly developing economy. Positions of wealth, considerable at times, and corresponding positions of elite status and power are being filled by persons who have no claims to such eminence other than those of political influence. Under the conditions prevailing in Nigeria at the time of independence, a very crucial source of influence and power could be found in a cabinet post, a top-level administrative position, or even a relatively subordinate position as long as it carried some political influence. Thus, a person may be posing as an administrator and may be classified as such in a superficially conducted elite study; but, in reality, he has already long reclassified himself by a shift of his own personal power bases from the administrative apparatus to the economic and financial scene. Through the influence of his office, he may have acquired a string of apartment houses, shares in a corporation, and the like, and it will only be a question of time before he changes over entirely to his new status. At the time of independence, the opportunities for Africans to acquire elite status based on wealth through their access to political sources of power and influence were increasing enormously. Sometimes, influence is also derived from control over substantial segments of the population—the youth, certain tribes, trade unions, and where they represent a force, traders and market women. Sources of that kind are short-lived; they produce recognition and political rewards only as long as there is political value in mass support—only during the stages when votes count and rulers are in need of support at the polls.

Political power derived from influence in a mass party—at least during the pre-independence stage, when positions of influence were being prepared and secured—depended more often than not on the benevolence of the colonial regime. It appears to this writer that it is erroneous, therefore, to treat leaders of political parties who rose to leadership during the colonial period as products of the power of charisma without taking into account the power of the colonial administrators, who, in most instances, could make or break an African politician. Most African leaders in Nigeria, from the Sardauna in the north to Awolowo, Azikiwe, and the legion of lesser members of the new elite in the southern regions, are the products of colonial politics, of choices made by colonial rulers from among a group of competing claimants.*

The usual pattern has been that, at the moment of transfer of formal power, the colonial rulers left behind a well-entrenched, hand-picked elite, even a cadre of a counterelite. These groups are small if compared to similar groups in more developed countries. The new elite is endowed not only with legitimacy—or the means by which it may be attained—by the departing rulers, but with the political power and influence derived from such legitimacy through its identification with the mutually agreed-upon constitutional structure. Others not formally placed in government and administration are endowed with starting power through a variety of nongovernmental devices: Some are made partners in the production processes, some in the distribution system, some in the financial sphere. This applies to the new commercial class, the managers, principal clerks, and administrators of the government-owned and operated enterprises. Some are given status through

---

* Perhaps the early Azikiwe is the exception to the rule, possibly the product of another imperial lapse.

education and training in the colonial mother country. The majority, especially in the southern regions, are concentrated in the urban centers.

Generally speaking, the Nigerian elite—not necessarily those directly participant in the rule itself—are weakest in their stability value in these respects: As a group, they are too small, too isolated from their following, too atypical, too transient, too loosely organized, and too inexperienced to withstand the stresses and strains likely to be encountered during the initial phases of independent existence. They still lack the "intensity of perspectives," the deep-seated attachment to values required for sustenance in the political struggle for power. They are not generally well-rounded. Some of those who may be well-educated lack adequate property; many of those who are wealthy may be either totally or partially illiterate; those who possess status through the traditional system alone may lack access to the instruments of power in the modern state; and those who possess formal power may be subject to humiliating treatment by those who occupy positions of power in the traditional social structure, especially in the north.

Another source of weakness lies in the area of legitimacy. To what extent will the people—for practical purposes, the second and lower elite levels—respect as valid sources of authority and legitimacy the positions of power and influence that result only from the direct exercise of power or from the indirect intervention by the colonial regime or its post-independence representatives? Will those who started late to acquire their education, their professional skills, and their economic power be willing to remain inferior to those who obtained a head start merely because they were deemed acceptable by the colonial rulers or merely because their families had been privileged under the colonial regime? Will the positions of economic power—those with access to points of control over means of production, distribution, etc.—be respected by those who started late? Will the fruits of wealth acquired under colonial rule be respected by future rulers? Will the system of government be deemed legitimate, and will the political positions, the laws, the directives, and the administrative rules be respected?

The top of the social structure is occupied by two types, the old, increasingly less effective traditional rulers and the new, increasingly more effective group. One exception is the north, where, among those identifiable as effective rulers, are, of course, the traditional elements. Among the latter, the Fulani-Hausa, the Moslem rulers, occupy positions of pre-eminence. Unlike traditional elements elsewhere in Nigeria, this group is strongly entrenched in the essentially feudal social-economic structure of the region, bolstered and supported rather effectively by the representatives of the colonial regime, even after independence. They clearly were the declared favorites of the Colonial Office, and are now favored by the Commonwealth and Foreign Offices. Drawing upon the spiritual and secular strength inherent in Islamic institutions, beliefs, and perspectives, the Sultan of Sokoto, the Sardauna —who, at independence, also served as the northern premier—the emirs, and their associates in the regional regime are well-endowed with the means required for self-perpetuation in power, barring, of course, an effective, massive intervention or internal upheaval. Because of the built-in predominance of the Northern Region in the federal scheme, the power of the northern ruling group is extended to the federal level as well. Yet, by reference to stability indices developed by Lasswell and Lipset, among others, the stability value of that group should actually be rather low.

The northern system generally does not favor political and social development of progressive social thought. The dominant idea system is a barely adjusted medieval-feudal one. Among the rulers, there is a pronounced lack of comprehension and appreciation of the great ideas that have motivated people in the past and that now propel vast masses toward change and revolution not too far from the Northern Region. There is a marked disinclination to engage the mind—their own or those of their subjects—in progressive social or political thought of the twentieth century. Indications are that the northern traditional rulers, as a group, are ideologically immobile and that this immobility interferes with their ability to develop the perspectives that could sustain both them and the masses through the pressures and tensions being generated throughout the north and, in fact, throughout Nigeria. As a group, they seem unable to perceive the futility of feudal rule. If the masses, at independence, seemed to be sustained by the predominant idea system, specifically by the perspectives shared by the rulers and communicated to the masses by the *mallams* and other opinion-directors in the region, it is only because of the stern, tight rule exercised, because of the absence of effective guarantees of human rights. Archaic methods of administration and archaic concepts behind those methods are not productive of perspectives of high survival value, or of high stability value, in the latter part of this century.

Given a favorable social and political environment, the elite recruiting system developed in the north is rather effective. It permits a certain status mobility at the top with a minimum of dissent. The inner discipline governing the northern elite is remarkable indeed, although it should not be understood that there is no dissent at all. But the environment will not be favorable much longer. The introduction of universal franchise—however restricted in practice in the north—tends to interfere with the prevailing elite recruiting system because it introduces legitimate alternatives for claimants to positions of power and influence. The availability of new sources of wealth, education, and training in administrative skills, no matter how circumscribed and ideologically restricted, will interfere with traditional methods of elite recruitment; the obsolescent and overly ritualistic political processes of the feudal regime lack the guarantees for responsibility required of the modern administration developing at the federal level. The reform of the penal code, undertaken in 1959, strikes at the roots of the recruitment system by undermining the political-juridical influence of the feudal rulers.

Where the claim to power rests on these factors, rulers depending primarily upon spiritual values are subject to overwhelming pressures in transitional societies. Given the opportunity to isolate the region, or at least portions of it, from the corroding influences of the south and the outside generally, the emirs and their associates may be able to sustain themselves through identification of their rule with Islam's religious value system. But it will be progressively more difficult to isolate the masses from the outside and to prevent them from perceiving contradictions between their own vital interests and those of their rulers. As the economic interests of the masses, primarily the peasantry or *talakawa,* clash with the precepts and tenets of the spiritually oriented feudal system, the focus shifts from the spiritual to the secular realm. At the time of independence, few substantive developments in the north indicated an adjustment by the northern rulers to the requirements of political survival under conditions of progressive secularization. On the contrary, there seemed to be current the belief and the conviction that militant opposition to reform and social change was an effective means of survival. But the interests ordained as legitimate and proper by the feudal regime became increasingly irrelevant in the struggle for existence, for corresponding opportunities were being provided for oppositional elements by commerce, technology, and education to create at least an atmosphere of challenge. Although Islam appears to be expanding in numbers, it is very doubtful that rulers who base their claim to power on Islam alone will be able to retain their positions in areas farther below the Sahara.* For Islam here lacks the strength of Islam in the North African area. Sub-Saharan Islamic structures generally are far more susceptible to challenge and corrosion, partly because of the inherent superficiality of adherents but also because, in an area such as Nigeria, the locale of economic power during the formative stages of the new state lies substantially outside the areas of greatest influence by Islamic control forces. This remains true despite the predominance of northern representatives in the

---

* For present purposes, little value is attached to performance claims by the northern rulers as publicized in speeches, public relations releases, and other communications of that sort. Most of the "achievements" claimed by the northern rulers should properly be credited to the colonial authorities and other non-Nigerian agencies.

federal government and despite northern control of the groundnut crop. As a matter of fact, it is more than likely that one effective challenge to the traditional rulers will emanate from the group representing them at the center, partly because the latter will be quicker to recognize the signs of decay and obsolescence than their relatively backward regional superiors. It is likely that the challenge will be couched in nonsecular terminology: Islamic reformist elements, for example, will assert that the traditional rulers' claim to power lacks validity because they have subverted the tenets and values of Islam to their own frequently corrupt purposes.

One of the prerequisites of stability cited by Lipset is the combination of power plus legitimacy.[2] The northern traditional rulers have at their disposal religion, which, under certain conditions, is also given high stability value as an instrument of power. The primary reason why the identification of rulers with religious concepts and practices enhances their value to the masses in Northern Nigeria is the fear among the masses—partly, of course, inspired—that competing religious forces represent threats to their security. Christianity is said to be a source of social unrest and instability because of its attitude towards polygamy, for instance. The emirs may thus buttress their claim to rule by referring to their value as defenders not only of the faith but of the prevailing social order, in the interest not only of themselves but of the mass as well. However, as pointed out elsewhere, this source of power and authority will not long survive economic development with the attendant introduction of new values, the class struggle, and other innovations.

While on the subject of traditional rule, a brief consideration of developments elsewhere in the federation may be appropriate. The tribal rulers as a group, most prominently the traditional rulers of the Western Region, have long ceased to be capable of ruling without secular support. Only where supported by either colonial forces or by indigenous nontraditional groups are they capable of performing functions significant in the power processes.

Where they are reduced to relying on the resources of tribal rule, the symbols and instrumentalities of chieftaincy, they rate extremely low on the scale of stability values: They can neither be relied upon to provide stability in their own behalf nor can they mobilize social or political forces to secure their rule, and thus the structure, against secular challenges. Frequently, their rule can be terminated by the stroke of a pen wielded by a half-educated politician, and the foundations of their rule can be undermined and destroyed by economic or political sanctions applied by secular forces without too much effort.

As the functions of the chieftaincy are separated from the person of the chief and are transferred to other secular officials and offices, the chief, the king, the *oba,* or whatever his title may be, is reduced to the role of a supernumerary in the administration. Neither he nor the institutions and processes with which he is identified, or which are associated with his office, can remain fully functional under these circumstances. He becomes a relic of the past, incapable of performing the role expected of him by his followers and by those relying upon him for executive performance. For a brief time, the chief and his traditional system of government are permitted to compete with the secular system. "Two lines of legitimate authority are competing on the local level for mass allegiance. The secular system will come out on top sooner or later. . . ." [3]

Traditional rule has stability value in the modern setting only if based on sources of power and influence other than traditional ones. In recognition of this, a few alert traditional rulers have "retooled" socially, economically, and politically to enhance their vanishing appeal and authority. The northern emirs decided to create a political party of their own to implement their decisions and secure their rule. The training of an indigenous cadre of northern administrators and skilled technicians, as well as of professionals—all, of course, loyal to the traditional rulers and dependent upon them—was recognized as another means of increasing the chances of political survival. Moreover, some of the traditional "royal" courts experienced the aforementioned face-lifting, and the ceremonial was spruced up and given a slightly modern appearance. Legitimacy is secured once more, but under a modern disguise. In this respect, the northern rulers are more advantageously situated than their western counterparts, for the former have at their disposal the means required for the modernization process, and thus can effect the process in accordance with their own precepts should they retool to become modernizing autocrats. Their southern counterparts, on the other hand, must defer to secular elements.

Economic power is also marshalled toward the retention of power. Access to the "rain-maker," or the witch doctor, as an instrument of control over the tribe and the community suffices no longer; power must be enhanced by such modern sources of influence as money and credit, employment opportunities, and other aspects of the matrix of social and physical existence. Thus, a new type of traditional ruler emerges: the chief-trader, chief-contractor, chief-planter, chief-banker or real-estate owner. In view of the controlling value of land in the matrix of existence, the control of land-tenure is crucial. Where land-tenure is under traditional control, as is the case in the north, stability is greatly enhanced, provided traditional rulers apply this factor with the requisite skill to the political processes.[4]

In brief, traditional rulers who rely solely upon spiritual and traditional means of influence for the defense of their power positions, or who rely solely upon ethnic loyalties in their tribal roles, will not survive long under pressures from the secular modernizing forces. More modern, more effective instruments of power must be acquired. The control of land-use, and the production of wealth tied to it, gives those who are skillful enough the opportunity to survive politically, at times even under the most modern conditions. The Yoruba aristocracy, perhaps more than its northern counterpart, has succeeded in exploiting this advantage, at least temporarily.

Along with control of the material aspects of power, traditional rulers desiring not to abdicate their roles are also being advised to equip themselves with legal counsel. As has been demonstrated so dramatically in Ghana, the secular forces, in their eagerness to undercut traditional, conservative elements, move in on the legal front. Causes for legal action against traditional rulers and their associates abound in systems that recognize no legal delimitations for governmental action, no systematic budgeting, and no book-keeping; that regard as customary and entirely permissible what the modern legal system regards as criminal; that rely on favorit-ism rather than on merit in their public employment and pro-motional practices; and that generally do not fit into the legal-constitutional structure because the latter was designed without reference to the social bases of traditional rule.

Countless traditional rulers also find modern politics difficult to cope with. The intrusion of extraneous forces and issues evoke reactions that may have been rational under traditional rule but lead to confusion, conflict, and instability under modern condi-tions. Increasingly, groups contending for power tend to bypass the traditional ruler in matters of substance, permitting him to play a purely ceremonial, symbolic role, provided that he does not embarrass those who use him. More and more frequently, tradi-tional rulers find themselves caught in the cross-fire between two or more groups seeking positions of power and influence in the area. As their capabilities to perform useful functions as arbiters, conciliators, and judges decrease, their value as rulers decreases. It appears that the traditional rulers in the Western Region have been drawn into the whirlpools of politics, have long ago lost their symbolic independence, and are surrounded not by bearers and recipients of chiefly power but by spokesmen and manipulators of local, nontraditional, conflicting interest and pressure groups. Many traditional rulers, in other words, especially in the southern parts, have become tools of the secular forces intent on replacing them as soon as they are no longer of any real value.

Added to the foregoing difficulties, suspicion is widespread in nationalist circles that the surviving chiefs frequently survived only because they were acceptable to the colonial power. This affects their claim to legitimacy in the eyes of the modern nationalists. The politics of "indirect rule" certainly contributed to the impression, for under that system only those chiefs were permitted to play a significant role who submitted to the will of the alien power. The source of the power and legitimacy of those chiefs lay outside the sphere of traditional rule.[5]

Another source of conflict and instability arises from the fact that in the Northern Region, the traditional rulers do not as yet fully recognize or completely accept the new secular authorities created and legitimized by the colonial power. This holds true despite the fact that the new authorities were brought into existence at a time and in a manner favorable to the preservation of traditional rule. The emirs accept authority derived from the regional or federal constitutions only up to a point, beyond which they regard it as no more than power delegated by them and subject to their ultimate control. They do not acknowledge the claims of the new legal authorities to prestige value. When possible, they demonstratively oppose the accrual of such value; they jealously guard their own prerogatives in key areas of rule by denying secular rulers access to such areas as court ceremonials.

One of the major decisions confronting the secular rulers of Nigeria, and of nearly all Africa, relates to the future placement of traditional rulers in the modern nationalist framework. A new formula for the utilization of chiefs must be found to replace the one employed by the colonial power; what is required is a twentieth-century version of indirect rule, an African version. If it is assumed that stability value, and other values as well, can be associated with a continuous-role performance by the traditional rulers—and it has been argued that the objections to such a solution are impressive—then a process is needed that will produce a traditional aristocracy of enlightened orientation, modernized, streamlined, yet representative of those aspects of traditional rule that have high stability value socially, politically, and psychologically. If modern secular African rulers can succeed in retaining some useful social values of certain select segments of their aristocracy, they may demonstrate a statesmanship superior to that displayed by their European counterparts.

It appears that, short of substantial secularization, modernization, and the general streamlining of the system of traditional rule in the north, only their identification with the dominant Moslem religion endows the rulers with stability value in the modern setting. If Islam is assessed as a major stabilizing factor in the rapidly developing country—and this is by no means certain or subject to universal agreement—the emirs have no effective rivals, for they monopolize the elite and leadership positions in that hierarchy. Indications are that the role of Islam as a stabilizing factor is strengthened where new ideas and practices are demonstrably incapable of providing security and stability. In this lies the strongest argument supporting the claim to leadership, at the federal level, of the emirs' party, the Northern People's Congress. In the southern regions, the Eastern Regional Government has so thoroughly politicized the already weak traditional rulers there that one can no longer regard them as independent factors. In the Western Region, a few select *obas* still exercise influence and power, but the institution as such has passed into the political realm, the center of gravity of which lies outside the sphere of traditional rule.

Those Who Provide

In the south, two major groups may be identified among the effective rulers: Those who derive their positions from the colonial regime and who, therefore, tend to have vested interests in the perpetuation of certain practices, relationships, and institutions; and those who are self-made, who rose to power through political action and agitation in opposition to the colonial regime. It is submitted here that, regardless of the source of power, the effective rulers in Nigeria at independence were the products either of direct British intervention and support or of tacit, indirect approval and support, no matter what appearances may convey.[6] Among the rulers, it is submitted, those who are less visible but who provide or control the means of wealth, the capital, the land, the facilities for production, extraction, distribution, and processing are pre-eminent. This applies to an increasing extent even in the north, especially as the pressures upon the feudal system there increase in competition with the rest of the federation. It involves both expatriate and Nigerian—although the former more than the latter—and both public and private ownership and operation.

Both Chief Obafemi Awolowo, the leader of the Action Group, and Dr. Nnamdi Azikiwe, the effective, though not nominal, leader of the NCNC, as well as a handful of other similarly developed political leaders, appear to be outside the group just referred to. In actuality, they are extensively and personally involved in the economic processes of the respective regions and of the federation as a whole. As long as they remain responsible and committed to the orderly development of Nigeria, their sources of power are severely circumscribed and restricted by processes and forces not under their control. It is, of course, conceded that both of these former premiers possess personal qualities that set them apart from the mass of lesser leaders and notables in Nigeria and that do, or did, permit them to achieve a certain degree of political independence. However, for present purposes, Awolowo and Azikiwe are exceptions, and an evaluation of political stability in Nigeria may proceed without special consideration of these two otherwise outstanding leaders. More important, more crucial, in fact, for our present purposes, are those who provide and control the material means by which Nigeria is and will be run. Here, of course, consideration is restricted to elements and forces present on the Nigerian scene at independence, for a massive injection of United States influence, or of influence from other non-British quarters, would, of course, introduce new factors.

As in most societies, the focus of the power struggle is upon shares of the wealth and upon the instrumentalities of control over the production and distribution of that wealth. In Nigeria, where indigenous private enterprise still is in its infancy, except for petty trading, the sphere of combat for conflicting interests lies in government control and the operation of the major income-producing sectors. Among those, for some time to come, the agricultural sector will be the dominant one. In 1959, it provided 85 per cent of Nigeria's exports. Therefore, that segment of the country's elite that derives power and influence directly or primarily from control positions in the production processes—on a large scale, that is; not for local consumption—and in the distribution or sale of agricultural products is likely to be prominent in the power structure. The leading products thus defined included, at independence, oil palm products, groundnuts and derivatives, cocoa, rubber, and cotton lint and seed. Great expectations concerning other products had not yet materialized, although plans were afoot to further diversify agriculture. In this setting, the government-operated marketing boards played a key role, and those on the boards who controlled policy decisions wielded immense powers. The boards had total control over the purchase and export of most products listed above, and the share of the national income controlled by the boards rose steadily.* Concerning the marketing boards, the following comment may be of value here: "An important feature of the marketing board system widespread in West Africa is that it confers on the board power to decide who may produce and who may not. It can, for instance, use its power to encourage indigenous merchants to become licensed or to encourage producers to set up their own marketing cooperatives, thereby ensuring them a 'double-take' first from the sale of the produce and then from the servicing of it. On the whole, this power has been employed beneficently up to now, but in monopolies, whether government or private, the dividing line between good and ill is hard to see and is therefore in constant danger of

---

* It might be pointed out here that the bulk of Nigeria's agricultural production represents the output of millions of farmers operating by totally inefficient methods. Even so, control over the purchase and distribution of the income-producing share of the output is concentrated in relatively few agencies.

being crossed." [7] It is suggested here that the lines are being crossed in several directions and that the boards have already become instruments in the struggle for power. One major weakness in the system, at independence, was that the elements controlling the boards were still primarily expatriate interests.[8]

As a matter of fact, as the second year of independence began, expatriate interests still remained in control of essential segments of Nigeria's economy, particularly of the distributive trade, road transport, and banking.[9] Increasingly, complaints were voiced, in and out of Parliament, that the destiny of the country, in spite of attainment of political freedom, actually remained firmly in the hands of expatriate groups, and was subject to decisions in London, not Lagos.[10] The fear was expressed that so-called Nigerianization of business concerns, even of the public services, was a bogus operation to conceal continued domination of expatriate elements.[11]

On the whole, relations between British interests—such concerns as the all-pervading United Africa Company, a subsidiary of Unilever, John Holt's, etc.—and African elements either representing them in Nigeria or dealing with them in government, administration, or private businesses have been good and are conducive to increasing constructive collaboration. This is, in no small part, the result of historic developments that go back several centuries. As a result of a long-standing association between British sea captains and merchants, on the one hand, and Nigerian chiefs and their representatives, on the other—primarily through trade—the economic and social benefits were passed on to what in time became a Nigerian middle class. In later times, the colonial administrations, as well as private British trading interests, were understood to be cultivating these roots until the emergence of a substantial—by African standards—indigenous elite presumed to be competent enough to assume many of the lower-level responsibilities of local self-government. Even after independence, though, British private interests dominated the economy and the power struggle focusing upon it; certain phases of the economy either drifted or were transferred into Nigerian hands. This applies to such sectors as real estate, rubber, cocoa, timber and lumber, and building construction.

In addition to promoting a Nigerian trader and small-business class, the British engineered the emergence of a Nigerian manager class as well. At first, this was done only in subsidiary, subordinate positions in an understudy capacity; lesser officials were placed in government-controlled enterprises, production and marketing boards, and development corporations. Likewise, private concerns, such as the United Africa Company and several French, Swiss, and other non-African concerns, to mention only a few, cautiously eased Africans into subordinate managerial positions. Gradually, a Nigerian economic managerial group materialized with a distinctly British slant on things and, what is most important for present purposes, with a vested interest in retaining the basic ingredients of what for them represented a rather attractive cooperative venture.[12]

Since the British were in control at both ends of the economic seesaw—in government-controlled and operated statutory public authorities and agencies, and in the private sector, especially with regard to export and import—the struggle for a share of the pound sterling from Nigeria was essentially interfamilial. The prospects of independence and the resultant pressures for the transference of controlling positions to Nigerians ("Nigerianization" of policy positions) injected new factors into the balance. Now elements whose support bases were outside the sphere of direct influence of the Colonial Office, the Governor-General's office, and the headquarters of expatriate firms appeared on the political horizon with forces behind them to lend weight to their claims for a share in the economic and power pies. Mass-based political leaders had to be appeased—or, perhaps, bribed. More and more of these new claimants and contestants for power had to be admitted into the heretofore select circle of the socially and economically powerful, primarily to assure fair, if not favorable, treatment for the expatriate firms and for the British interests in general. Because the established pattern had been strongly monopolistic—partly to protect the interests of the indigenous population against predatory adventurers from non-British areas—a wedding between the British interests and the new Anglo-Nigerian elite was indicated from the start. Government, business, and politics were part of the same power pattern.

Because of the close, even statutory relationship between what in Nigeria may be designated "big business" interests and the federal and regional governments and their agencies, which are oriented toward economic issues, political opposition becomes of necessity opposition to the rulers in general. Under such conditions, the convenient fiction so essential for the operation of Western democracy—that political factions compete under the umbrella of a benevolent, neutral government—is destroyed. The entire legal, constitutional, and formal political structure becomes the butt of elements convinced that they were "dealt out" when the structure was arranged and entrenched. Much of the resentment will, of course, be directed at the British expatriate firms, no matter how much good will they attempt to secure with selected investments in the development of the country. Likewise, the other non-African elite elements—the Lebanese, Syrian, Greek, French, Swiss, and other trading interests—will be subjected increasingly to extreme pressures and hardships.[13]

For some time, efforts have been under way, substantially supported by U.S. foundations and government projects, to develop, on somewhat of a crash basis now, an economically independent, viable Nigerian entrepreneurial class. One concept behind this is that of the vital role of private economic interest in the successful operation of Western democracy. It is hoped of that group that it will develop the capabilities of a challenging force on the political scene, offering vigorous and effective opposition to the government and its allies.[14] In view of the likelihood that the weaknesses of the industrial sector in the Nigerian economy will endure for a considerable time, the continued dependence upon monopolistic practices in the larger agricultural sector, through combines of

Nigerian businessmen-politicians, Anglo-Nigerian managers of state enterprises, expatriate interests, and partisan politicians, appears to be indicated.

Yet the effects of political independence, and of the growing complications on the international scene, are bound to weaken the bonds between the British elite and their Nigerian partners. In theory, the upstart contenders for power could increasingly resort to the legal, parliamentary, and administrative instrumentalities at their disposal, thanks to universal franchise, in order to improve their power positions, if nothing else. Then, those who have been in control of the key strategic points in the economy, and of the colonial-influenced power structure generally, would become comparative outsiders, separated both from the channels of formal power and from numerous effective levers of everyday politics. Those who would then control the formal machinery of government would be the effective rulers. If this were to come to pass, much agony and strife might be avoided. However, the established elite has several levers remaining at their disposal: control of export and import, and, thus, of the life-lines of Nigeria; control of likely sources of capital supply; control of those aspects of international trade that are of direct and vital relevance to Nigerian survival interests; and, finally, bribery.[15]

A pattern already is discernible. Unscrupulous but skilled politicians, having been lifted into positions of influence through the electoral processes, seek to exploit the newly gained positions of strength for personal advantage. The squeeze on foreign enterprises and interests has been on for some time, and it is being tightened continuously.

Aside from the fact that by such practices an important resource of the Nigerian people is being misused—namely, the power to improve the common good—the effect of such developments is to sap the strength of the not too healthy social, economic, and political structures. In the interest of both foreign and Nigerian business and industry, and in the interest of economic and political stability, a political bargaining machinery must be found to permit foreign interests to generate adequate political pressure to bring their views to bear on key governmental and political personnel at significant points in the control machinery without having to incur extra expenses unrelated to the purposes to which they are committed economically. Because foreign capital is required for the development of the country, foreign interests must be reasonably protected against predatory forces employing political blackmail. Fairness in contract-letting, for instance, is unlikely to be achieved without effective restraints in law and in politics. In this connection, it should be noted that there exists in business circles in Nigeria, as elsewhere in the underdeveloped world, a fear of the effects of a possible intrusion into the economy by Soviet Russia, Red China, or both. These forces, government-controlled and regimented, with little or no commitment to the maintenance of existing structures, arrangements, and practices and with few ties to the prevailing economic interests, could further unsettle already unbalanced relationships within Nigeria.

Thus, under the conditions prevailing shortly after independence, it is difficult to see how the indigenous economic elite can be evaluated highly in terms of positive contributions to political stability. They do not seem to possess the economic or political wherewithal to secure stability through the enforcement of established rules and concepts. The forces arraigned against the economic elite are formidable: The late-comers, who believe that an allocation of wealth, power, and influence has been made while they were either not looking or not in position to make their claims felt; the extremist nationalist-oriented groups, who are convinced that the Anglo-Nigerian elite is but an extension of the colonial influence; and the political parvenus, who press claims for shares of the national wealth based on mass support.

Aside from the fact that a large percentage of the economic elite has long been composed of expatriates, or persons closely identified and associated with that group, the indigenous economic elite has produced few individuals who may be assessed as politically independent. "The need for self-help is not understood by the African businessman who looks to the Government, and the Government alone, for financial assistance in the expansion of his business, instead of going with others, in a partnership or other form of common enterprise." [16]

Thus, if political stability requires, among other things, a change in accordance with established rules, powerful forces are convinced that these rules discriminate against them in the struggle for a just share of the national wealth. As for the dominant group, they have a vested interest in the retention of most of those rules, of the substance of the legal-constitutional structure passed on to Nigeria by the colonial power, of the parliamentary institutions and practices of like origin, and of general Western rules of political behavior. But because they do not represent a force separate and distinct from the government, but are, instead, closely identified with it and its goals and purposes, they tend to become standing provocations to opposing factions. Under those conditions, political change, through election or parliamentary processes, is not likely to produce results acceptable and satisfactory to the malcontents. For the latter—groups preferring rules free of restraints against social change or revolution—the political struggle will be conducted increasingly outside the grounds designated by the Anglo-Nigerian elite. For some time to come, the ruling element within the economic elite—the segment controlling the production of wealth and the means of distribution—are firmly entrenched; so, too, are the controllers and suppliers of capital, backed as they are by the political, legal-constitutional, and coercive apparatus and by the opinion-influencing media, both traditional and modern. It is primarily the lack of genuine, effective competition, the lack of adequate bases for individual enterprise and initiative, and the social and geopolitical imbalance that render political stability in Nigeria so precarious. The social and geopolitical imbalance, however, will be adjusted as progressive southern businessmen, managers, directors, planters, distributors, and financiers develop a sense of impatience with the rulers of the north and their preoccupation with the maintenance of the traditional status quo.

Ministerial Associates

One group associated with the ruling elite can readily be dismissed as having relatively low stability value, largely because its positions are primarily nominal and derivative. That group contains most of the cabinet ministers at the federal and the regional levels, their associates, and, in general, the personnel who make up the formal regional and federal governments of the day. With too few exceptions, they derive their positions from association with individuals and groups not part of the formal structure. Most of them lack the prerequisites of power: access to the means of production of wealth, to the means of distribution of wealth, and to the coercive apparatus. Most lack sufficient familiarity with the intricacies of administering the modern state to be able to utilize the many opportunities—and the many that are opening up as the country develops—for acquiring private wealth, independent power, and influence. Most lack the basic skills required to translate the prestige associated with their nominal positions into substantive political power. The majority of the regional and federal ministers are helpless adjuncts of the civil-service hierarchy and the forces in control of the economic apparatus and system. In the north, most ministers and ministerial secretaries and functionaries are putty in the hands of the traditional rulers. As one observer put it: "What does one expect of a minister who throws himself into the dust when encountering the emir? What respect does such a person command among the voters and people in general?" Likewise, what influence and respect can a politician command who is intellectually incapable of making decisions in his own domain and relies wholly on the support and judgment of expatriate administrative officers?

As in the case of traditional rulers, vulnerability to corrupt influences materially affects the stability value of this group. The practice of giving presents to chiefs, judges, and public officials is a time-honored custom. The giving and receiving of "customary presents" can be regarded as institutionalized practice in Nigeria, particularly in the north. The eradication of this practice is exceedingly difficult, partly because those who would have to take the lead in the elimination of the practice are also its chief beneficiaries. Close observation indicates that many cabinet officers and lesser ministerial functionaries concentrate much of their effort and time on searching for opportunities to accumulate private wealth. Successful or not, such pursuits by numerous ministers seem to be encouraged by many of their subordinates; the latter seem to prefer to keep their ministers preoccupied with nonadministrative matters in the interest of efficiency. The relative inability of many cabinet ministers to secure private gain from public office finds some compensation in the willingness and ability of commercial firms, African as well as European, to offer bribes; the combination produces an unsettling situation with regard to official functions at the cabinet level.*

Several of the regional and federal ministers, it must be noted, as well as some of the ministerial associates, possess the educational qualifications, among others, to perform the duties of their offices with a high degree of competence. Individually, they represent towers of stability, but the system of which they are a part tends to produce more officials of the type described above. Some of the more capable individuals have already amassed sufficient wealth to qualify as politically independent powers in their own right. But it appears that many a fully qualified Nigerian, during the early stages of self-government and independence, displayed

---

* In 1959, in the Western Region, an anticorruption officer functioned in the regional government. However, the competence of that officer was restricted to cases that were expressly brought to his attention by the cabinet, *i.e.*, the premier. Thus, virtually no cases could be, or would be, investigated unless the party leader had decided that a man needed to be challenged. Anticorruption activities under such circumstances represent primarily another disciplinary weapon at the disposal of the party and government leader.

a great reluctance to consider the possibility of serving in a governmental capacity. The norm of conduct at the cabinet level, and perhaps in government and administration generally, was then such that persons brought up with high standards of personal behavior were not particularly attracted to such service. Under the circumstances, this amounted to a considerable drain on the country's already strained resources.[17]

The People's Representatives

The essential meaning of representation is difficult enough for people in advanced societies to grasp. So is the meaning of the responsibility of the governors to the governed. No matter how highly developed traditional modes of representation may have been, no matter whether forms of responsibility existed with regard to the rule of chiefs and elders, the conditions under which modern parliamentary government operates are radically and materially different. The relationship between the citizen-voter and the governor-ruler is quite different, for it is only with great difficulty that the average African voter, illiterate and uneducated, can fathom the meaning and utility of the system for his own existence. Superimposed on this matrix of problems is the British practice of representation, which does not require that the representative reside in the constituency for which he is to speak.

In areas where the moral and legal restraints are at a minimum, the waiver of residence requirements tends to encourage corrupt practices and irresponsibility. Constituencies, along with other alien institutions and practices, then become but a means to personal ends; a parliamentary representative is then likely to view his constituency as a fief of sorts, and his political career is not necessarily tied to it. Given favorable conditions and ample opportunities, the income from corrupt practices in his constituency may be substantial enough to make him independent of voters anywhere in the country. He may then retire from politics to become an influential businessman. The only safeguards, under the circumstances prevailing at independence, were moral, ethical, and social commitments not to take advantage of the opportunities offered to a person with influence in a developing country. It is an understatement to say that such commitments simply have not yet materialized to a significant extent in the political process.

For many, a stint as parliamentary representative constitutes the first opportunity to emerge from tribal—or, sometimes, slum—existence. They either are successful in politics, use politics to fashion a nonpolitical career, or sink back into poverty and obscurity. The loss of a parliamentary seat means more in Nigeria than in advanced societies: the loss of an opportunity to improve one's material standards of living. Under those conditions, many parliamentary representatives can be expected to devote considerable time to providing material insurance against the time when the opportunity has dried up.[18]

Generally speaking, politicians and parliamentary representatives in Nigeria today should be given a very low stability value on intellectual grounds alone. Far too small a percentage are intellectually prepared to grasp the essential aspects of the representative processes. Among those who are adequately prepared, Nigerian talents are second to none. The overwhelming majority, however, are neither equipped to comprehend the constitutional and political processes underlying the parliamentary institutions of which they are a part nor committed to defend the letter or the spirit of the law. There is no reason to believe that they would be capable or inclined to offer meaningful, effective resistance to a determined assault on the constitutional system by forces intent upon subverting it by legislative stealth or overthrowing it by frontal assault. Among them, individuals with a vested interest in the preservation of the broad outlines of the constitutional system are too few to prevent a scramble for survival in a revolutionary situation. In such a situation, then, the parliamentary representatives cannot be counted upon to act as a stabilizing force. This situation is heavily accentuated by the fact that too many of the truly qualified, skilled, and morally directed persons remain aloof, on the political side lines, awaiting the end of the uncertain and, to them, distasteful period of transitional politics. Politicians as such do, of course, have a vested interest in the survival of the society that enables them to attain positions of influence and power; they have a stake in the efficient operation of key aspects of that society and in the general validity of the rules by which the political game is played. But they do not have a stake in stability, in general, largely because their interest is not so much related to the advancement of the basic, vital principles of democracy as to the acquisition of wealth and the attainment of status and prestige. Since the 1950's, the tendency for wealthy politicians, however, is to retire from direct participation in the more time-consuming and precarious partisan-dominated political process, leaving the field to the lean and hungry teachers, clerks, trade-union officials, small businessmen, local-government officials, lesser administrators, scribes, and the flotsam and jetsam of society.

A word might be added on the subject of political party functionaries and similarly occupied association officials. In a setting where parties like the dominant northern party, which was the victorious party in the 1959 federal election, lack nearly all known characteristics and instrumentalities of party and party function, officials and functionaries as such cannot be expected to occupy too significant a place in the power structure. Where party organization has been developed to a high degree of efficiency, as, for example, in the western Action Group, party functionaries are wholly under the domination of the leader. Neither they nor the functionaries of the numerous associations, voluntary and other, are sufficiently well-entrenched, politically, economically, socially, to deserve a high influence rating. This has been especially true in the Eastern Region, where the organizational principle applied to the party by the leader—in this instance, to the NCNC by Dr. Azikiwe—for a long time required the installation of mediocre functionaries in key positions in preference to potential challengers of the leader's authority. In that respect, the north is not much better off. As pointed out elsewhere, if the requisite skills are present, political positions can, and frequently are, parlayed into private wealth, hence power and influence.

In summary, perhaps the greatest threat to the native rulers emanates from the fact that they attained their positions of power and influence, including the means by which they rule, under a regime controlled and imposed by aliens; that the source of their legitimacy was alien; and that the political philosophy behind the regime of which they are a part was the product of a colonial system that had entered the stage of obsolescence. In the north especially, the leaders who control the land, the means of production of wealth, and the channels of distribution are too closely identified with imperial rule to subject themselves and their group successfully to a thorough political metamorphosis. Control points in the economy elsewhere in the country—the control of mines and industries, of commercial and financial establishments, of key posts on marketing boards and on boards in control of other state-owned enterprises—had been secured under the imperial regime before progressive, democratic African forces were in a position to share in policy determination. Rulers identified with this system of allocation of bases for power must be expected to be challenged by spokesmen of groups not represented in the crucial earlier stages. Only to the extent to which the post-independence African rulers are capable of manipulating their power to the end of meeting the demands of the masses for concrete evidence of advancement under independence will they be able to protect their positions. Yet their close identification with the departing or departed colonial regime, particularly pronounced in the north and only a little less so in the west, presents an obstacle to a successful identification with the aspirations of the rising African masses. The failure to produce real gains will force them to fall back upon control of the means of coercion and persuasion. A skillful use of these means, under favorable circumstances, may postpone the counter-elite's day of reckoning by reducing or minimizing the challengers. But the army—however small in numbers—police, and other agents of control are devoted to the rulers only to the extent to which the latter can fulfill their aspirations. At the outset, under the colonial regime and during the period of initial independence, membership in the apparatus of coercion has economic and social prestige value. As the economy develops, as living standards improve, and as demands increase correspondingly, that value is reduced, and the ability of the rulers to enforce their will is also reduced. The rulers can more readily be separated from the protection that is provided by the dependency, which in turn stems from the income and living-standard gap between them and their most essential supporters; the degree to which the latter become cognizant of the gap determines, to a considerable extent, the degree of loyalty at the disposal of the ruling group. In the north, the emirs have much to fear in that respect.

It is by no means certain what kind of images the Nigerian masses hold concerning the role, function, and value of their leaders. What kind of leadership do they prefer? Assertions that the concept of chief-ruler is dominant among the masses are untested. Perhaps preference points to a modernized version of the traditional ruler? But how far can he be modernized without taking him out of the social and political milieu of which he has been, and perhaps must be, a part? Charisma may be the element that, if combined with the other functions of the institution of chieftaincy, will produce a useful modern adaptation. David Apter in his examination of policy in Ghana seems to think so.[19] Lerner observes: "The main alternative to the rule of personal charisma, in this phase of rapid modernizing, is probably the reign of terror." [20] Nigeria, at the time of independence, had shunted onto a siding, temporarily at least, its most likely candidate for charismatic rule, Dr. Azikiwe. He had been transferred, or maneuvered, from the purely political role of regional premier to the more ceremonial and symbolic role of governor-general. Perhaps he would issue forth with renewed vigor, armed with the prestige gained from the symbolic but exalted position perhaps as the first President of a Republic of Nigeria. For the moment, his chariot had been sidetracked in favor of leaders less charismatic, less antipathetic to the prevailing system of rule. If developmental tasks confronting the new rulers prove to be beyond the means available to them during the first few years of independent existence, as is likely, the pressures for the abandonment of the remaining vestiges of the nominally democratic form of government will mount. Then, when terror should be the only alternative, charismatic rule could prove to be the superior solution. Sentiments are widespread in some elite circles that it may be far wiser to anticipate the disintegration of the state and society by taking corrective measures at once than to wait until events have gone too far.

Ruling groups confronted by pressures such as those being generated on the economic, social, and political fronts in Nigeria, must, if they wish to avoid violent change, devise methods of elite recruitment designed to inject into their ranks quantities of superior intelligence, vigor, and modern skills. The prevailing methods of elite recruitment, however, are not yet such as to bring the ablest, most talented, and most skilled young men and women to the top. Here, too, the north suffers more than the other regions. Yet technological requirements alone are such as to encourage the production of greater numbers of graduates of secondary and higher institutions of learning. Soon, dissatisfaction with society's evaluation of their capabilities, as they themselves see these, can become one of the most potent sources of political instability; for the rulers entrenched under the colonial system prefer to place these people in accordance with their own politically sensitive scale of values rather than merit. Although this may, for the moment, be a politically more secure utilization of skills and talent, it will be a constant and powerful source of rancor, dissatisfaction, and revolt in a setting where almost any kind of modern skill or advanced knowledge has prestige value far above that encountered in more highly developed societies.

5

The Working Elite and the Enemy

Some Must Think and Plan

Like the rulers, the bureaucrats must represent value to the masses. As operators of the machinery of government, they are most visible to the public and are most directly in contact with it. If interests intent on bringing about changes in state and society are willing to attain their objectives in accordance with the accepted formulas, they must have confidence in the bureaucracy. Where such confidence is lacking or inadequate for proper public-administrator relations, extralegal, illicit, conspiratorial, or outright revolutionary methods and tactics are favored by oppositional elements.

Two interrelated factors stand out among those helpful in determining the stability value of the Nigerian bureaucracy: the nature of the relationship between Africans and Europeans, or other non-Africans, and the element of Nigerianization. At the time of independence, neither the rulers nor the principal bureaucrats had arrived at a settled policy for their mutual relations. Perhaps the major stumbling block was created when an attempt was made to superimpose upon Nigeria an administrative grid based on insights and principles developed in Britain in the period following civil-service reform and during the period of stabilization of social and political conflicts there. Nigeria itself was perhaps not yet ready for the advanced type of bureaucracy that the colonial advisers and social engineers had brought to that part of Africa. Although the British are concerned with strengthening the integrity and efficiency of the bureaucracy and with separating the bureaucracy from political partisanship, the African rulers view the administrators very much as their predecessors did in Britain prior to the reforms: They expect the bureaucracy to be a tool in the power processes, including those outside the limits of legality, propriety, and legitimacy. Thus, in spite of all the formal declarations and the paper pronouncements, the bureaucracy is expected to be instrumental—or, at least, not to be an obstacle—in the acquisition of individual power or of group power. Objectivity or impartiality by the bureaucracy in the power processes is not appreciated under those circumstances. The truce, evident during the periods immediately prior to and following the attainment of independence, may well be broken as individuals committed to the British system are replaced by Africans otherwise committed and subject to economic pressures by elements intent on harnessing the administrative services to their own ends. In view of the scarcity of competent personnel suitable for employment in the administration, it should not be too difficult for interested groups to subvert bureaucrats to their ulterior purposes.

On the surface, relations between the departing Europeans and the Africans are conducive to stability. Unlike other areas in Africa, Nigeria does not have to contend with a white-settler problem and the impact of that problem upon civil service and administration in general. The colonial officials themselves are on the way out, and those remaining are changing over to a different relationship based on contract rather than imperial prerogative. As progress has been steady in the replacement, or Nigerianization, process, confidence in the genuineness of the arrangements being made between the colonial power and the Nigerian elite has, of course, been considerably enhanced.

In favor of stabilizing trends in the bureaucracy is the development that sees long-frustrated Africans moving into positions of responsibility after a seemingly hopeless struggle against prejudice. For too long, top government executives, including African ministers and members of parliament, as well as leaders of industry and business, have lacked faith, perhaps understandably, in the ability of Africans to perform adequately in positions of responsibility. The Parliamentary Committee on Nigerianization summarized the problem quite succinctly: "To very recent times, ministers, parliamentarians, and public men of this country had lacked faith in themselves, lacked faith in the African Civil Service, and had regarded every expatriate civil servant, no matter what his qualifications or experience, as an expert. The Nigerian, no matter how highly qualified, irrespective of any experience he might possess, was never accepted as an equal of the lowest and least experienced expatriate." [1]

Under the pressure of events, this spirit has rapidly been supplanted. Ready or not and experienced or not, Africans have been pushed into advanced positions while Europeans have been retired.[2] Although the effect of this development on the morale of the Europeans has been severe in view of the rapidly diminishing numbers of expatriates, this fact alone cannot be evaluated as significant in the determination of stability potentialities in the administration or bureaucracy—unless Africans fail to perform adequately and substantial numbers of non-Africans must be reimported. At the same time, it must be pointed out that many expatriates, particularly the younger unmarried ones, who can afford to take a chance with the new Nigerian rulers, appear to have adjusted themselves careerwise and psychologically to the African social and political climate. In some instances, expatriates have so thoroughly identified themselves with their new masters that they have come into conflict with expatriates in other parts of the country or elsewhere in the British Empire or Commonwealth. For instance, very strong loyalties have developed among expatriates serving in the several regional governments, and those serving at the federal level not infrequently are at odds with the former on matters of policy, particularly where the interests of the regional rulers clash with federal preferences.

Another factor indicating a stabilizing function on the part of the Europeans is related to the high value placed by Africans on the Europeans' arbitration capabilities. To the extent to which Europeans remaining in Nigeria, and in the bureaucracy in particular, are able to identify themselves with the new rule and with the basic aspirations of Nigerians, their service as arbiters in internal conflicts, especially tribal and ethnic conflicts, will be highly valued. In certain conflicts involving their survival interests, Africans have good reason to fear their own people more than they may have to fear Europeans. Where Ibo will promote only Ibo, where loans and contracts are extended only according to the degree of ethnic or tribal affinity, and where members of an African official's tribe receive automatic preferential treatment in his sector of government service, the European presence frquently is regarded as a safeguard against injustice and discrimination.

However, a dichotomy between the prevalent British and the African-Nigerian concept of the role of the bureaucracy in the political process exists, and it tends to widen the gap between principle and performance as Africans replace Europeans in key administrative posts. Even before independence, it could be noted that Africans willing to observe the rules laid down in the colonial service were beset by doubts whether such conduct really was in their own best interest. It is most difficult for a rule-abiding civil servant to accept an increase in his work load as a result of preoccupation by a superior or colleague of equal rank with unofficial activities for private gain. It certainly affects the morale of personnel within range of knowledge of such goings-on. Where practices of that kind become the norm, the stability value of the civil service in terms of its performance capabilities is, of course, substantially reduced.

Within the African complement in the bureaucracy, tensions do, of course, develop—not only along tribal lines, but also on the usual grounds: The few who have attained positions of high responsibility are overworked and believe themselves fully qualified to take over the jobs of their superiors in rank. Large numbers of older Africans, who built up seniority in the service in relatively subordinate positions under the colonial regime, consider themselves fully entitled to rapid promotion, but they find that younger interlopers from the universities and technical institutions, as well as those who are direct products of the power-political processes, move into relatively superior positions. Meanwhile, because they have not acquired the intellectual tools and formal prerequisites for advancement, they are frozen in their lower-echelon positions. They do not recognize, or will not acknowledge, their technical shortcomings, if any, but will instead, as is the custom, tend to emphasize the value of their seniority standing. And as has been pointed out elsewhere, there always exists the temptation to acquire interests extraneous to those related to official duties, especially while the country is moving ahead at a dizzying pace and fortunes are being made by individuals commanding no more intelligence and no more skills than some modestly compensated civil servants nailed to a position of inferior rank and low responsibility.

Still another source of conflict and instability potential in the role of the bureaucracy in the Nigerian Government is created when politically minded leaders recognize the inherently conservative tendencies manifested in a British-trained corps of civil servants. Impatient to seize power completely, politicians, particularly the ultra-Africanist variety, regard bureaucratic concepts of orderly and systematic administration as subversive when these methods tend to delay the total power take-over.[3]

A constantly shifting formal governmental and societal framework will require an extremely farsighted and skilled personnel policy; a narrow conceptualization of the role of the administrative services and related aspects of public policy can prove disastrous in a country where so much depends upon the proper functioning of that aspect of government. During the periods of transition, the few remaining expatriates and small number of African bureaucrats with minimum qualifications will be operating under severe pressures and handicaps. Given no settled personnel policies, doubtful career alternatives, dim social security and retirement prospects—excepting those expatriates who were and are paid handsome lump sums upon retirement from the Nigerian service—few administrators will be able to concentrate entirely on the professional tasks before them. It is clear that the public services and bureaucratic sectors at the federal level, as well as in the several regions, require substantial regularization before conditions can be said to be reasonably stabilizing.[4]

What applies to the federal and regional administrations and to the bureaucratic hierarchies at those levels also applies to the local-government staffs throughout Nigeria. British tutors practiced what had taken centuries to develop in counties at home under the close control and supervision of the British gentry and aristocracy. The rulers at home, however, were deliberately slow in conferring significant instruments of power upon local-government bodies, as they were slow with regard to universal suffrage in general. For reasons discussed above, the educational training and waiting periods—the periods of apprenticeship for local government—had to be drastically curtailed in the colonies. A major fork in the road opened up: Was local government to be used to train Nigerians for democracy? Or was democracy to be introduced from above? A British secretary of state saw the problem in this light: "I believe that the key to success lies in the development of an efficient and democratic system of local government. I wish to emphasise the words efficient, democratic, and local; democratic because it must not only find a place for the growing class of educated men, but at the same time command the respect and support of the mass of the people." [5]

But the system under which gradualism would have made sense, that of colonial rule, was crumbling fast; new rulers were taking over, and new national goals required new methods. The slow and leisurely methods of traditional African government, which permeated local government everywhere, were inadequate if not critically dangerous: "A man has only one life and it is idle to expect an educated African gentleman . . . to fritter away his efforts in arguments with yokels around the parish pump." [6] Even the more advanced methods of British local government rapidly became, in effect if not in intent, obstructionist, because those methods, to be effective, required too great an emphasis on formalities, local consent, and gradualness.

Local-government concepts and practices developed under fundamentally different conditions simply are not applicable to the conditions Nigeria will have to cope with for the foreseeable future. The system as operating at the time of independence simply was not capable of conducting the social, economic, and political reforms that were needed. Ideally, people develop the most meaningful concepts of democracy only with respect to their own local-government authorities and institutions, and the personnel administering local affairs ideally should be closest to the will of the people. But not enough persons had been trained prior to independence to operate local authorities satisfactorily, and there was not enough time left to conduct a training program with an emphasis on the development of democratic concepts and practices based on local requirements and experiences. Top political leaders, African as well as British, became impatient with the relatively slow processes below them and in the field. African leaders also suspected that British commercial and political circles, both in Nigeria and in London, preferred local-government autonomy for better control of the indigenous population.

It appears that, in spite of the recognition of some of the difficulties, a decision as to which fork of the road to take has never been made. Local government in Nigeria now suffers from ambivalence and ambiguity, among other things. Considerable confusion is created by the plethora of conflicting expert opinions now being spread around by Polish, Indian, American, Israeli, and numerous other foreign advisers employed by the several governments. Although many policy makers still seem to be devoted to the ideal of utilizing local government as a training ground for democracy, the same people, primarily the planners among them, actually reduce all chances for such a development. In their impatience to move along, or as a result of a sense of panic, they choke the communications channels between themselves and lower echelons with avalanches of conflicting, mutually contradictory directives. Too frequently, they render a method or a concept obsolete before it has had a chance to be comprehended and thus integrated below. Too frequently, there is no time to ex-

periment and to test an idea since a new, wholly different idea
has already been incorporated in a set of contradictory directives.
Personnel at the local level, as a result, are not encouraged to
apply themselves to the tasks before them with a sense of purpose
and continuity. Too frequently, they deal with predominantly
illiterate, tradition-bound local leaders and groups; as a result,
they cannot act with as much dispatch and precision as may be
expected of them by top policy planners and directors. The result
frequently is that higher levels ignore local-government authorities in their quest to get things done. Aside from creating confusion, such practices tend to discourage the more able and more
competent among local-government officials, many of whom entered local-government service with a sense of mission. These
people, some of whom are superior in education and general
qualifications to many of their regional or federal superiors in the
governmental hierarchy, resent being reduced to, and used as,
errand boys.

Under these circumstances, it is small wonder that neither the
public nor the personnel staffing local-government institutions
seem to develop a feeling for one another; the people, as Cowan
noted, harbor a strong element of doubt and confusion as to the
legitimacy of the new organs of government, organs that are
demonstratively at the beck and call of nebulous power centers
above and beyond the familiar horizon. Cowan sees a real confusion as to the foci of authority and loyalty derived from the
juxtaposition of traditional and modern secular systems and institutions.[7] If one considers further the impact of yet another
juxtaposition, that of regional-secular versus local-secular authority superimposed upon the picture presented by Cowan, the consequences should become clear. When and if local groups become
reconciled to secular local authority and begin to cooperate, the
political quarrels between partisan political centers at the regional
level—to which local authorities are constitutionally responsible—
and differently oriented partisan political groups at the local level
soon negate whatever has been accomplished.

The introduction into local service of political protégées and the interference in local affairs by political parties concerned primarily with the power struggle, and less with the development of local responsibility, tend to subject local government to severe shocks and jolts, which only the most determined, purposeful, and firmly supported local authorities can cope with. In addition, the inadequate checks and controls against corruption and mismanagement should make local authorities degenerate rapidly into political cabals fighting for survival with any and all means at their disposal.[8] The successful local-government servant, under those conditions, will likely be more of a political hack than an administrative expert.

The practices of recent years in all regions, but primarily in those where local authorities tend to come under the control of political parties other than those in control of the regional government, and thus of the ministry of local government, indicate a disturbing pattern. Conditions that are aided, abetted, and influenced by regional political-power centers are made the pretexts for political intervention from above, not primarily for the purpose of correcting malpractices below but for discrediting a political party identified with a specific local authority. Official inquiries are instituted against municipal or other local-government authorities, and the local authorities are dissolved or suspended. Whatever the result of such actions, the local bureaucracy stands to be discredited, no matter how efficient, loyal, and devoted to the principles of local government and democracy it may have been.

As is the case with the federal and regional bureaucracies, inner tensions over goals and methods, ranks and seniority, status, and career outlook beset local-government personnel. It will be some time before every group within the administrative hierarchy has developed a working concept of a smooth, mutually beneficial relationship. In times of severe crisis at higher levels, regional as well as federal, local authorities in some countries possess sufficient acumen to carry on, maintain vital services, and generally hold the country together. Although local-government personnel are being trained at reasonably well-run schools and institutes, and although some of the local officials are of superior caliber, local government in all three regions cannot yet be counted upon to serve as a stabilizing factor in a revolutionary, or near revolutionary, situation.

Some Must Do

Aside from the personnel equipped with the administrative bureaucratic skills required to operate governmental institutions and to assure the execution of both public and private policies, there is a need for sufficient personnel equipped with specific technical skills (including organizational, communicatory, etc.) to hold state and society together and to assure order and continuity. On the surface, Nigeria appears to be as well-equipped in that respect as other underdeveloped countries. However, if one excludes expatriates, the problem becomes apparent in its full magnitude. At independence, the country did not have technically skilled personnel in numbers adequate to guarantee stability under conditions likely to develop shortly after independence.[9] The planned and projected training program, both domestic and overseas, promised to produce greater numbers under a marked acceleration of the recruitment and training efforts. Yet one of the major problems remains, and will confront policy planners for some time to come: the great expansion of the sphere of responsibility of all governmental and private agencies. For example, the demands for technical services before independence were but a fraction of the demands generated by a public delirious with promises associated with independence. Increased private activity, of course, also necessitates the expansion of the public services.

Although a reliance on mere numbers will always be inadequate for qualitative assessments, this is particularly true of the evaluation of a country's technical and administrative resources. Mere figures tell only part of the story. Assertions that Nigerians, or Africans generally, are inherently and biologically incapable of acquiring advanced technical skills are, of course, nonsensical.

There appears to be no scientific basis for allegations of that kind. However, it can hardly be argued that advanced technical skills can be acquired by a society without extensive and protracted cultural, psychological, and educational preparation. Nigeria is too close to primary stages of social development to have already produced the foundations for the production of an adequate body of competent technicians. Individual cases are often outstanding in terms of performance capabilities, but the gap between these few and the majority of Nigerian technicians is not reassuring at this time.

Thus, technicians generally, whether in industry, commerce, or, above all, the public services, will for some time to come have to be supplied from non-Nigerian sources. If not of British origin, then they may be of Israeli, Indian, or other noncolonial (Western) origin.* A fundamental problem opens up. How can a political system operate successfully if the key technical services are performed by foreigners? What is the state of internal security if the majority of key technicians, scientists, and experts are subject to outside loyalties? How do rulers assure compliance with their policies and directives? How do they obtain guarantees of loyalty and devotion from foreigners performing highly sensitive, skilled roles in society? To an extent, the terms of the contracts under which foreigners are performing their roles supply leverage to their employers. But the essence of loyal service is enlightened self-interest, or even an identity of interests between the individual and the society he serves. From that standpoint, Nigeria cannot hope to obtain reliable commitments from technicians hired from abroad. The stability value of this group among the elite is limited and is further reduced as its share of the total available technical personnel increases. Not only does such an increase tend to aggravate the tensions associated with Africanist aspirations, but it might endanger progress in general because of the popular antipathy to measures either executed by foreigners or associated

* In time, of course, Communist-bloc technicians may be introduced in large numbers.

with foreign influences.[10] Science and scientific progress in general, to be popularly accepted, may have to be brought to the masses by Nigerian contact persons, and foreigners may have to be kept in the background, restricted to relative anonymity.

In the last analysis, those technicians who have mastered the skills required for the effective operation of the armed forces and of the police occupy the most sensitive strategic positions next to the rulers themselves. Lasswell notes that, because they are so strategically located, "control over violence is the most firmly entrenched, hedged about with the severest sanctions and most rigid perspectives; in particular it is the most tenaciously held to by the elite, least subject to concessions." [11] The British colonial regime did not part with nominal control over the instruments of violence and coercion until shortly before independence, and then only because it was assured of continuous control by elements deemed responsible from the British point of view. At the crucial 1957 Constitutional Conference, the subject was broached, and it was agreed to transfer control of the Nigeria Regiment from United Kingdom control to the Nigerian Federal Government as of 1958. Even then, transfer of control meant primarily transfer of financial responsibility. The control of the police was transferred to a more substantial degree before independence, but, again, only because the political balance of power and general circumstances were such as to render impossible any use of the police for purposes unacceptable to the joint British-Nigerian group of rulers.[12] It can be said that well beyond independence—as had indeed been foreseen—the established Anglo-Nigerian elite enjoyed a monopoly of power over the means of coercion by keeping out of the hands of the elected representatives any essential aspects of control over armed forces and police. In this design to secure power and stability, the latter group was aided by the pressures generated by intra-Nigerian regional and subregional conflicts that militated against any attempt to vest control over the more sensitive instruments of power in locally directed bodies.

It appears certain that once the remaining British controls are

either substantially weakened or wholly removed, the instruments
of coercion and of violence will be subjected to the hazards common in underdeveloped areas generally. They will then be open
to subversion in the interest of domestic as well as of foreign
groups by bribery, propaganda, or appeals to tribal or personal
loyalties. The Nigerian rulers and vested interests will, of course,
seek to postpone this day as long as they are permitted to by the
more militant nationalists.[13]

Tending to enhance the stability value of the police and armed
forces' functions, in the context of political stability, is the fact
that the British, quite unlike the Belgians in the Congo, constructed a Nigerian armed force and a police force designed to
serve the Africans rather than the Europeans alone. These forces
were selected and trained to produce efficiency, loyalty, and striking power. This policy has paid rich dividends, at least during the
initial periods of independent existence. The major weakness in
the Nigerian armed forces may be that they are proportionately
too small for the population of Nigeria and that expansion, which
must be commensurate with the rapidly deteriorating situation on
the continent in general, must of necessity be conducted without
the benefit of strict and impartial British supervision. If carried
out by politically oriented persons, in terms of local partisan politics, for instance, the achievements of the original British tutors
may be watered down substantially. The new, enlarged army may
then be less immune to the hazards of subversion than could be
said of the British-trained cadre. The same is essentially true of
the police.

Police control and administration in Nigeria will, for some time
to come, suffer from these defects:

1. The principle of federal, or centralized, control of the police
runs counter to the principle of federalism as conceived in Nigeria
at the time of independence. In fact, the principle of central police
administration and the principle of federalism are incompatible.
Enforcement of the law through a federally controlled police
tends to aggravate divisive tendencies in the federation. Yet to

regionalize the police is to provide each region with a militia to be used against the other two or three in the event of conflict—and conflict is inherent in the structure. Also, regional police administration would lend itself to enforcement of policies detrimental to the interests of tribal minorities in the several regions.

2. Once British personnel are withdrawn and the balance has shifted to non-British controls of the police, either Africans or foreigners from noncolonial countries will be the controlling elements. In either case, it will be most difficult to locate personnel with a clear, unequivocal, and undivided commitment to national security.[14] Whereas in colonial days, and even shortly after independence, the directors of the police force, although expatriates primarily, shared fully and unreservedly the interests of the Anglo-Nigerian elite, the new directors may have conflicting loyalties.

3. Local authorities subject to the stresses and strains of transition, with respect to personnel, and financially less and less able to cope with the increasing demand for services, will become progressively less able to perform the local police function.

Silence is Gold

The fourth estate in Nigeria has as yet not developed positions of power. Like the elements referred to in the foregoing chapter, this group lacks prestige, influence, and positions of power, partly because it lacks the skills required for survival, partly because it lacks the motivation and the economic means to secure an independent status. At the time Nigeria attained independence, the press substantially depended for its existence, as an industry and as far as individual members of the profession were concerned, upon the forces controlling the regional governments, which, in turn, employed the medium for its own purposes. Generally speaking, and overlooking the relatively petty and insignificant quarrels between cabinet ministers, politicians, and lesser elements on the one hand, and the press on the other, one may safely say that the fourth estate was a captive in Nigeria. Expatriate or Nigerian, publisher, manager, editor, or writer—all were more or less subjected to economic and resultant political pressures to conform, in significant respects, to the dictates of the ruling groups.*

The concept of an independent, critical, and responsible press, which is deemed necessary for the operation of free Western political institutions, is entirely alien in a setting that traditionally has seen only fully integrated communications processes. Moreover, freedom of expression runs counter to the demands of the developmental machinery that governments must set up and operate with reasonable success in order to survive. Neither the federal nor the regional governments can be expected to tolerate criticism in the only major communication media available; but where criticism is permitted, it will not be viewed with favor by those who rule if their positions and their sources of influence and power, as well as their modes of conduct, are open to public discussion. At independence, the leading press personnel were either overly cautious expatriates controlled by the desire to stay in business under difficult conditions or Nigerians, mostly captives of political organizations or cliques. Men and women of great potential talent are among these groups, but most confine themselves to rather irresponsible pamphleteering on matters related to imperialism, colonialism, and, in the domestic sphere, trivial political sensationalism unrelated to the more salient political processes, issues, or personalities. Much of the so-called political press represents journalism of the worst variety; it does not even make the pretense of research, investigation, and verification. Because of the extreme dependence of the working press and the supporting staffs upon the good will of the several governments and political-power groups, the press cannot be expected to play a significant role in the balancing processes associated with orderly, systematic, rule-

* One of Nigeria's most able and most prominent journalists, referred to earlier, told this writer that he had chosen to concentrate on foreign affairs rather than domestic politics, which had been the basis of his reputation until then, because "one never knows who will be boss tomorrow."

abiding change. It will not challenge the established order on legitimate or on other grounds unless ordered to do so by its political superiors. Nor will it resist illicit, improper, and otherwise objectionable activities if these are part of the political-power complex. Especially in the several regions, the press appears to be wholly captive and compliant unless its political "bosses" find it desirable and expedient to utilize it for purposes of challenging the rulers in a competing section within the federation, in the federation itself, or in an opposing group within the region. To that extent, some competition exists in the press sector, but it is inherently unrelated to the press function. It is related to the political-party propaganda function and thus not designed to inform, enlighten, or educate.

Political conditions at the time of independence were such that it appeared highly unlikely that Nigeria would develop within the foreseeable future a corps of press personnel, newspapermen, publishers, and commentators who would defend what they considered to be the objective truth; who would be motivated not by political or private gain, but by the exposure of facts relevant to an understanding of Nigerian social affairs, significant political relationships, or the broad goals of moral and ethical behavior in accordance with generally acceptable standards.

Freedom of the press grows in direct proportion to the number of active participants in the political processes of a state, and Nigeria still has only a small number of such participants. Under these conditions, only those interests are articulated in the press that are in accordance with the wishes of the rulers. In particular, the executive and legislative branches of the several governments will jealously guard their prerogatives and will view with grave misgivings any group tending to compete in the opinion-forming sector of the political power machinery. A number of libel proceedings against members of the press in the several regions reveal the intent of the governors in that respect.

The foregoing should not be interpreted to mean that much of the Nigerian public would not greatly appreciate free discussion and analysis of vital questions. An analysis of the *Daily Times*, the paper which comes closest to the status of independence, reveals a consistent avoidance of sensitive issues, a preoccupation with the requirements of balance in the coverage of news from the three regions and the major political parties, and a reluctance to advance criticisms other than those officially inspired. Waste and corruption, for example, are discussed in detail only with regard to small, politically insignificant groups or, where politically appropriate, in connection with tribunal or court proceedings. In general, the most interesting aspects of the Nigerian press are the items of political import that are widely known but not published.

At present, if there is freedom of the press in Nigeria, it is largely a matter of the press in one region, under control of one political party, criticizing the government of competing regions and thereby the leadership of competing parties. To that extent, the federal system may be a guarantor of freedom of the press, up to a point. The Western Region—i.e., the Action Group—maintains the best news media in terms of journalistic standards, style, and contents (e.g., the *Daily Express* and its Western Region Television at Ibadan). The NCNC "house organ," the *West African Pilot,* which has never been a paper of high quality, has deteriorated considerably since the NCNC entered into coalition with the NPC. Primarily to counteract the negative influences of the regional press, in particular of the *Daily Express* and the other smaller AG-supported organs, and partly to enhance the prestige of the federal government against that of the regions, the *Morning Post* and *Sunday Post* were created to project the federal point of view, including, of course, that of the Northern People's Congress. Without these federal organs, the NPC would not be able to make itself heard as effectively in the rest of the country. The two *Posts* are under the Federal Ministry of Information. A federal television service is projected.[15] Needless to say, neither the federal newspapers nor the projected TV service can be expected to provide objective news coverage. These media are, in effect, propaganda arms of the federal government in its struggle to assert itself against the regional influences. The fact that it is propaganda rather than objective news coverage that is produced detracts from the safety-valve function—and thus from the stabilizing influence that could be wielded by a national press.

The Aloof Aristocracy

Among the blind, the one-eyed has distinct advantages. In a society still predominantly illiterate and socially ill-defined, fluctuating, and subject to alteration, a person with any knowledge of the law represents a power factor of considerable weight. As a group, lawyers in African society occupy a key position. They are an aristocracy, privileged, prestigious, and valued by the rulers as a support group. This applies to nearly all professional persons. The lawyers, nearly all British-trained practitioners of Anglo-Saxon law, speak a technical language that few, if any, of their clients understand, and the chances are that few of the court personnel can follow any but the most formalized terms. It is unlikely that many defendants or plaintiffs, in other than native courts, are in a position to break through the barrier of jargon and technicality, of legal concepts alien to their way of life, and to begin to understand what the lawyers are really talking about. Under those conditions, litigation can all too readily escape the control of the public and become an object of manipulation by an interest group; under those conditions, lawyers need only identify themselves, as individuals and as a professional group, with the regional or federal control groups and their spokesmen on the benches, to ensure relatively smooth sailing.*

It has been precisely because of the characteristics described in the foregoing that the northern rulers, and their representatives in government and administration, have steadfastly resisted the incursion of lawyers from the southern sections. In a setting such as

* The present Federal Minister of Justice, Dr. T. O. Elias, offers incisive observations on the subjects of law, the courts, and the legal profession in his *Government and Politics In Africa* (London: Asia Publishing House, 1961), Chapter 9.

that in the north, where widespread corruption and inefficiency permeate the entire judicial and administrative structure, a skillful lawyer can, without much expenditure of energy or funds, do the work of battalions of rioters or insurrectionists. The Action Group and the NCNC recognized the opportunities early: Especially around election time, squads of lawyers were dispatched from the headquarters of AG, NCNC, and affiliated groups to stimulate varieties of political actions in the north. No matter how powerful the northern local hierarchy was—and it fought back with equal skill and determination—nearly always a substantial amount of political static was created. Thus, in the minds of the rulers of the north, lawyers who are southern and non-Islamic have obvious revolutionary potentialities.

The major resistance to this group derives from African nationalist groups, members of which lack professional status, do not possess any particular skill, and do not share the same essentially Western values. Substantially oriented toward African culture, these groups view with misgivings the Western bearing of the lawyers, their social and professional connections, perspectives, and consequent political leanings. If a general trend should develop away from Anglo-Saxon jurisprudence toward new African frontiers, legal concepts, and practices, the legal profession will lose political footing and will move farther out on the political fringe. The exceptions will be those who compromise and who adjust their value system, their professional bearing, their techniques and skills to the preferences of the new rulers. The majority of the British-trained may be driven into either opposition or surrender, primarily because the legal-constitutional system to which they have been committed as a group will crumble away, first in regional practice and then altogether. The Westminster model will survive, in essential respects, only as the requirements of federal balance of power dictate. The legal profession, the judges, lawyers, and law clerks will have value under those circumstances. As the federal balance shifts—and it matters little in whose favor it shifts—the last vestiges of the value of British-trained members of the legal profession will disappear. Then, the British-trained professionals will, as a group, cease to have social and political stability value; if they themselves do not become members of the ruling elite, their purely technical skills will then be placed at the disposal of the new rulers. Where this occurs, political ends will have supplanted professional ends, and another problem will have arisen.

Because of their scarcity in numbers in the face of overpowering demand for their services, members of the medical profession can themselves determine their value to state and society. But where they take part in the political processes, they soon abandon their medical practice, or at least begin to neglect it. If willing to conform politically, they are guaranteed, as are the lawyers, professors, and other professionals, a secure place high in the social-prestige structure. Their professional interests, as a group and individually, cause them to be oriented toward the status quo, and they display distinct preferences for social discrimination against the masses starving for their services—where, that is, the latter are conscious of the advantages of medical science. As alluded to earlier, the pressure from actual and potential clients, in certain cases numbering millions, upon the few available physicians, surgeons, and specialists is so immense and so unlikely to be met within the foreseeable future that arbitrary practices of selecting and treating patients must be, and are, applied. The preferential treatment of the socially, technologically, and, therefore, politically valuable persons must remain the rule to assure a semblance of order and to assure minimum progress.[16] This places the medical profession on the side of the elite, in a community of interests of which they already are a part in their own right as professionals. Their stability value, wherever they are capable of exerting influence as a group, is correspondingly high.

A segment of the professional elite that commands significant respect and wields great influence in many countries is, of course, found among the leaders of the armed forces, the commissioned officers and, at times, the noncommissioned officers. Although Nigeria's armed forces are expanding, and although an African military elite already existed at independence, it cannot be said that this group was as yet strong enough, as a group, to play a significant role in the political power struggle. The same can be said of the officer corps of the federal police. The political potential of these officers is limited for a variety of reasons, one being their relatively brief history as a group. The majority of the Army officers have been commissioned only within the last two years.[17] Although they may have ideas of their own concerning the best possible way to advance the interests of Nigeria, they will for some time to come lack the economic and physical wherewithal to impose their will on the makers of political decisions. Their stability value in terms of the preservation of the prevailing system of government should thus be assessed rather high, much higher than that of military elite elements in certain other developing areas, primarily because of their comparative political impotence.

The Nigerian intellectuals generally appear either to be headed for the political sidelines or to be embracing oppositional precepts. Where illiterate traditional rulers are in control of the machinery of government and of the instruments of power, this development should not be surprising. Likewise, where illiterate or semiliterate politicians are either in control or in the ascendancy, intellectually oriented persons cannot be expected to enjoy participation in the political processes, especially where the processes are mired in corruption and inefficiency. The difficulties experienced by this group appear to be traceable to the same causes everywhere in Africa: Nearly all its members have been trained either in Europe or at European-oriented institutions in Africa, and they may be more correctly described as Europeans in black skin. Some efforts are under way, in western Nigeria especially, to produce an intellectual group steeped in African culture, but the results of this effort will not make themselves felt for some time to come. Meanwhile, as a group the intellectuals tend to be either oppositional or apolitical, leaving politics to the rapidly rising bourgeoisie and the nationalist-politician classes. As everywhere else, there are some outstanding exceptions.

The Enemy Within

Lasswell and Kaplan identify as a likely source of instability the countermass and the counterelite. To them "the countermass is largely drawn from the subject classes, to be sure, but may also contain segments of dependent classes (for instance, intellectuals), and in crisis situations even comprise parts of the ruling class. Similarly, the counterelite is recruited from even higher intervals on the scale of value positions." [18] Lipset warns against false analogies in that respect; he appears to think that the patterns that applied to revolutionary situations, and to opposition politics generally in Europe, do not apply in Africa.[19] This idea seems to be borne out: In Nigeria, the traditional aristocracy, the upper bourgeoisie (Anglo-Nigerian, in the main), the landowners, and even significant numbers of the ruling secular politicians, on attainment of national independence, overwhelmingly subscribed to ideological propositions incapable of generating loyalty among the masses. This was quite unlike the comparable development in Europe. As in most of the emergent states, the predominant ideological patterns in Nigeria were of alien, Western origin; they clearly bore the stigma of subservience to colonialism.

On the other hand, ideologies of the political Left—Marxism, Communism, and Socialism, which are incipient in various sections of Nigeria—are relatively compatible, on the surface at least, with the goals of Africanism. They possess strong capabilities of appealing successfully to the masses. Potentially, especially during the immediate post-independence period, they have superior prestige value, if not among the Europeans, then certainly among the new post-independence aspirants to political leadership. Thus, social-revolutionary movements in Africa may find it easier to attain a relatively high degree of legitimacy compared with Western Europe in particular. There, these groups are compelled to operate on the legal, social, and political fringes, burdened by the opprobrium of treason, disloyalty, subversion, and sedition. Although the British-installed rulers in Nigeria, especially in the Northern and Western Regions, attempted to apply the same brush to their own brand of social revolutionaries, although they undoubtedly receive aid and comfort in this endeavor from other Western countries, they will find it very difficult in the long run to overcome the handicap of their own close identification with the sources of colonialism.

As has been pointed out above, oppositional tendencies are inherent in many groups, particularly the elite groups. Here we speak of the coagulation of such tendencies into an effective countergroup, preparatory to change, possibly revolutionary change. In a country like Nigeria, the ruling group, installed by processes determined by alien forces, faces a special problem. As soon as the independence celebrations were over, the masses represented by intelligent spokesmen began to seek an answer to the question posed by Lasswell and Kaplan—namely, what is the degree of realization of value of the elite for the mass?[20] The first severe test shaped up over the ability to live up to expectations raised by popular misconceptions concerning the consequences of political independence.[21] The multiplication of developmental tasks that becomes the political responsibility of an indigenous government is bewildering, often overwhelming. Inevitably, shortages, breakdowns, and frustrations occur; the public, uninformed, misguided, and often filled with bizarre, wholly unrealistic expectations, becomes restive, resentful, and overly attentive to the shortcomings and malpractices of the new rulers. Under those conditions, a counterelite will be formalized. Younger elements in the ruling elite and other strata, including some members of the police and of the officers corps of the newly formed armed forces, become impatient with the lack of dramatic progress, resentful of the apparently firmly entrenched and invincible traditional rulers, and suspicious of the British-created bureaucracy. At first, they will entertain thoughts of political change, then of rebellion and insurrection. Army officers and noncoms, the police and parallel ranks in the administrative services will all develop increasing dissatisfaction with the ruling groups over inadequate and what to them appear to be unjust methods of elite recruitment, since the younger, and frequently more competent, individuals must wait until the creatures of colonialism and the parvenu politicians have either died or been removed by slow, gradual means beyond the control of the reformers.*

The impact of the confluence of adverse transitional social and economic conditions and the lack of adequate restraints against corruption, mismanagement, inefficiency, etc., forces the intellectuals, the true nationalists, to become ready recruits for the counterelite. Three major groups may be identified among the counterelite in Nigeria: the conservative and reactionary, the moderate-liberal, and the social-revolutionary groups. Among the first, in all probability, are members of several Moslem sects or societies devoted to the attainment of religious-spiritual goals of Islam as interpreted by them. In all probability, members of the *Tijaniyya* sect are found in this category. Although the exact contemporary political goals of the sect cannot readily be defined—are probably unknown to outsiders—it appears to some observers that one fundamental goal is the return of Islam to orthodox ways, possibly through association with Pan-Arabism.[22] *Tijaniyya* may well be viewed by the rulers of Sokoto (a spiritual center of sub-Saharan Islam), of Kano, and of Kanem, etc., as a device for the more effective propagation of the faith in combat with alien and unstabilizing ideologies, doctrines, and practices. Installed by the methods of indirect rule, the Sultan of Sokoto and the emirs may form a counterelite against the leaders installed by the methods of representative democracy, incomplete as the latter system may be. This group resists the secularization of political theory and prac-

---

* It should be noted here that this writer sees no indications that oppositional activities of military and police personnel will be based on the organized instruments of coercion, the armed forces or the police apparatus. Instead, the personnel in question will act on an individual prestige and influence basis.

tice by invoking traditional religious symbols and myths, among
other devices. As the secular power at the center, and in the south
generally, gains momentum—through technological progress, for
instance—the traditional counterelite in the north may become
more virulent, more reactionary, and more determined to restrain,
to check, and ultimately to defeat the secular, popular-based
rulers. In the north, there are also elements favoring "a modern
state based on Islamic constitutional principles but adapted to
modern conditions. Relatively small in number and confused in
aim, they favor a democratic pattern of political authority with
Islam as the religion of the state." [23] Similarly motivated are the
indigenous fascists, also small in organized numbers.

Among the moderate-liberals, several groups may be distin-
guished. In the north, a group of relatively young men and
women, secularized by Western education, react strongly against
medieval versions of Islam and the superstitions interfering with
the performance of essential tasks in a modern society. "Islam is
scarcely vital to their thought, and in social and political fields
they recognize its implications only insofar as allegiance tends to
demarcate." [24] Mallam Aminu Kano and his Northern Elements
Progressive Union-Sawaba (NEPU) are the most substantial
forces in this group. For greater effect, if not for its very existence,
it is closely affiliated with nationalist groups in the south (at present, with the NCNC).

In time, an effective countergroup may emerge from a combination of the disillusioned intellectuals, nationalists, and such groups
as the trade unionists. A major revolt of taxpayers, wage earners,
and other similarly motivated groups could bring a coalition of
oppositional elements to the fore. In such a grouping would be
individuals who served in positions of responsibility in the early
stages of self-government, but who retired temporarily: some to
local-government posts, some to teaching positions, and others to
professional pursuits in medicine and law. These elements may be
described as leaders-in-waiting. They retired partly because they
disliked the widespread corruption, partly because they despaired

of accomplishing their assigned tasks under conditions so decidedly unfavorable. They recognize that the masses have been misled to believe that wonders could be worked upon attainment of independence, that they were filled with false hopes, and that they will now blame anyone who assumes responsibility under these conditions for what they must regard as leadership failure. They also are painfully aware of the drain on the country's resources by corruption, inefficiency, and waste. Some look to the workers for support because they regard the workers as being "incorruptible by their nature." Among these people, it is held that the workers and the farmers are the real losers in the transfer of power from colonial to corrupt and inefficient African regimes, although by prevailing standards the Western Region may be considered a model of efficiency. But as a direct result of British colonial policies, the workers are relatively unorganized and scattered as a group. Some of the liberals believe that, under their leadership, labor and some other disadvantaged elements can be aroused to form the nucleus of a truly nationalist movement to which would rally small taxpayers, farmers, and other underprivileged and generally harassed groups. The ideological orientation of these groups, at independence, was popular-democratic, with a marked appreciation of authoritarian measures to be applied to key sectors of state and society. A preference for democracy was perhaps only temporary; an endorsement of democratic procedures was based, in part, on the realization of these groups that an espousal of dictatorial principles would create conditions favoring one or the other of the major parties in operation at the time. Since members of the group with whom this writer came into contact seem to regard all existing major parties as being equally corrupt, they should be expected to be reluctant to give anyone the opportunity to close the door to the emergence of a reform party. It may well be that their ultimate goals cannot be attained without the adoption of dictatorial measures. The effects of corruption, inefficiency, and immorality are widespread, and it is believed in some of these oppositional circles that dissatisfaction based on these malpractices and weaknesses will in time mobilize substantial popular support for a "benevolently dictatorial regime."

Among the moderates should also be counted those leaders who fail to accept the existing political boundaries inherited from colonial days. Some of these are the Pan-Africanist adherents of West African federation, followers, or "parallel sympathizers," of Nkrumah. These people derive their sense of opposition from a feeling that the new rulers betray the higher cause of Africanism. The temper of this group emerges from its attitudes toward measures taken by the Ghanaian regime, even where such measures were directed at Nigerians in Ghana. They are sympathetic because they ascribe to Nkrumah motives similar to their own, and their concept of loyalty transcends that associated with "Nigeria." In part, their attitude derives from the conviction that governments like the one created by the British for Nigeria are mere extensions of the imperialist device of "divide and rule" and that opposition to such governments is therefore required of all true anti-colonialists. Furthermore, they share a dislike—a revulsion, in fact —of traditionalism and feudalism, and since both are rampant in the northern interior parts of virtually all West African territories, they conceive of themselves as members of a southern crossterritorial "international," an association of progressive transnational Africanists.*

One of the potentially most substantial sources for oppositional activity against the prevailing order exists as a result of the aforementioned continued expatriate control over the economy, the armed forces, the police, and foreign affairs. It is unlikely that the political rulers of Nigeria can do much about that in view of the fact that the country will not, for some time to come, command the capital, skill, or personnel resources to replace foreign interests. But the opposition in Parliament, at present represented by the Action Group, skillfully fans the flames of discontent among the

---

* It should be noted that liberalism in Nigeria need not be equated with democratic orientation, for, as has been stressed, even the moderates there reveal preferences for dictatorship. If these groups may be classified as "liberal," it is solely in terms of the theoretical ends they seek or profess to seek, not in terms of means they intend to apply once they are in power.

nationalists, the workers, and particularly Nigerians of moderate means, who believe that expulsion of expatriates—British, Swiss, French, Syrian, Lebanese, Greek, and other foreign elements—will provide enormous opportunities for personal acquisition of wealth. Certainly, if a minister in the Federal Government, the Hon. Waziri Ibrahim, has to concede in the House of Representatives that the government is powerless against the influence of expatriate interests, even one year after political independence has been achieved, nationalist sentiment is bound to be stimulated to seek relief.[25]

There remains the radical Left, the social-revolutionary element among the elite. As elsewhere in Africa, the roots of this and related groups are frequently found in European centers of learning or in the United States. In more recent times, East European and Soviet influences make themselves felt, even in relatively well-shielded Nigeria. Some of the leaders identified with the Left may be described as Marxists, some as Socialists, some as Communists; all appear to be Pan-Africanist, at least in principle. Many are students, full or part time, or former students. The centers of their activity are most likely found in schools and universities, in government, or in the directing bodies of political parties and movements. As reasonably educated and relatively highly skilled individuals, they are likely to enter positions of influence and prestige, bringing their political preferences with them. Because of this rather than because of their numbers—which, in fact, are insignificant—they must be reckoned with. Some of the radicalism found among members of this group may be ascribed to exuberance derived from a youthful devotion to ideals; some is generated by what they term anticolonialism; and much will, in time, mature to more balanced judgments, particularly with increased responsibility. But the element of radicalism is there, social-revolutionary preferences are shared by people in high places, and outside interests intent on exploiting these tendencies may do so as the opportunities increase. The continued and persistent predominance of expatriate interests in the economy of independent Nigeria tends to enhance the chances of the radicalism of the

Left becoming respectable. The same can be said of the frustrations born of the unwillingness of the ruling group to break the
financial bonds established under the colonial regime. The clash
of principles was well defined in an exchange between the leader
of the Opposition, Chief Awolowo, and the principal architect of
the private-enterprise–oriented post-independence economy, Chief
the Hon. Festus Okotie-Eboh, Federal Minister of Finance, in the
course of a debate on nationalization of basic industries:

> Chief Awolowo: "In the first place an untrammeled capitalist sys-
> tem, of necessity, places a newly developed and underdeveloped na-
> tion, such as ours, in a state of defenseless economic servitude and
> unduly prolongs the regime of poverty, ignorance, and disease among
> the bulk of the people."
>
> Chief Okotie-Eboh: "Experience in other countries has shown that
> quite apart from the loss of individual freedom and liberty, wide-
> spread state ownership and control do not necessarily lead to rapid
> economic development, nor to the material betterment of the mass of
> the people." [26]

Although sound economic reasoning may counsel against nationalization of the "goose that lays the golden egg," the desire to assume full control over the destiny of the country may yet push the
country down the road chosen by Guinea, Ghana, and others.
Chief Awolowo and his supporters may be playing with political
dynamite in their endeavor to embarrass the NPC–NCNC coalition government. Many observers think that the strength of radicalism of the Left is directly related to the reduction of northern
influence on the affairs of Nigeria. The slower the process of modernization at the center, the stronger will be the revolutionary impetus. In the first year of independence, the revolutionary Left
was well contained. Its representatives in such organizations as
the NCNC auxiliary, the Zikist Vanguard, or Dr. Azikiwe's impatient young men, had been educated to responsibility by a cautious leader, himself saddled with high responsibility and perhaps
sidetracked temporarily.* Other members of the Left, from the

---

* It will be interesting to see how these reformed "young Turks" will be-
have once they are forced to conclude that their dreams may have been shat-
tered permanently.

schools and universities, had either assumed positions of social responsibility in government, business—and those were rather few in number—or the professions, or been relegated to relatively un-important and safe positions. Some clearly appear to be in a kind of internal exile or rehabilitation condition while they await clear-ance to assume positions of prestige and influence. The Secret Service, still largely under the supervision of expatriates, was well in control of the situation, was well aware of the sources of radi-calism, both internal and external, and knew the principal points of contact with likely sources of ideological and financial support, both within Nigeria and in foreign countries.[27]

One of the first challenges posed after independence sprang from the dissatisfaction of elements in the organized youth move-ment with the performance of what they had considered to be "their" nationalist government, namely the NCNC group at the federal level. As the exigencies of coalition politics forced the NCNC ministers to defend rather than criticize the conservative policies of their northern coalition partners, radical youths formed the Nigerian Youth Congress in 1961. Because their objectives were well expressed by the opposition in Parliament, the Action Group, the leaders of the NYC themselves drifted into an alliance with the Opposition. Although the NCNC Executive Committee managed to bring most of the NCNC youths back into the fold at the end of 1961 by compelling key individuals to resign from the Congress, the fact that it was possible for youths from all parties to discover a common ground in opposition to the prevail-ing regime must have given the rulers food for thought.[28]

Until more dramatic developments fan the flames of radicalism —and developments in the Cameroons and the Congo, for exam-ple, are certainly disturbing and conducive to its growth—the op-position to the continuing influence of the northern feudal rulers is going to remain the most likely source for agitation by the revo-lutionary Left. The massive intrusion of foreign capital into the Nigerian economy, on terms reminiscent of colonial days, also tends to incite resentment, and the effects of spreading corruption and the like could, of course, also propel revolutionary elements into action. It should be recognized that continued rule by feudal elements in Nigeria will also be a most likely target for agitation by non-Nigerian forces intent on encouraging instability and creating chaos. Rather revealing in that respect was the following response obtained in an interview with a Moslem member of the oppositional Northern Elements Progressive Union in Jos, Northern Region, in 1959:

Q. "What do you think of the Soviet Union?"
A. "We hate Communism."
Q. "What is it with regard to Communism that you hate?"
A. "The killing of people without justice. The oppression of Moslems."
Q. "Do you see anything good in the Soviet system?"
A. "Yes. They destroy people like the emirs."

On the other hand, one should not underestimate as effective stabilizing, countervailing factors on the scene, particularly with regard to possible effects on radicalism and the revolutionary Left, those that are derived from traditional ways. Thus, the instability potential of radical groups—their revolutionary capabilities, for instance—may be substantially modified by countervailing forces derived from the conservatism inherent in traditional systems still dominant on the Nigerian scene, even though the systems are in the throes of change and dissolution. For example, students who affect Communist thought patterns, or who are Communists, will, upon return to Nigeria from abroad, encounter severe criticism from their relatives and associates. If one either has contributed to the education of the individual concerned or is related to him without having contributed, he is entitled, so it is believed, to material benefits—for example, a share in the earning capacity of the student. Political activity in a revolutionary sense is unlikely to lead to the kind of rewards envisaged and is therefore evaluated as an unsuitable preoccupation, a waste.

6

Groups: Popular Kaleidoscope

Patterns of Partisanship

In the social order of a territory in the developmental state of Nigeria, few groups, other than tribal groups, possess the organizational and moral cohesiveness of groups in advanced societies. Few cluster around value concepts that are modern and of reasonable durability under the stresses of transition. Nearly all groups are affected one way or another by the break-up of the old order, detribalization, and the dissolution of traditional patterns of existence generally. Nearly all of more recent origin address themselves to ephemeral issues, primarily of a compensatory nature, the focal point of such groups being the discovery or the organization of interests, values, and benefits that are to take the place of those lost as a result of social or other change. The social and political structures of Nigeria, at the federal as well as at the several regional levels, cannot be said to have as one significant component a firm, durable, consistent interest or value-oriented groups. Perhaps the most significant aspect for present purposes may be the fact that most groups operating in Nigeria today are provisional in terms of principal goal orientation.

Of the groups most prominently identified with political processes, political parties do, of course, occupy a key position, even though, in Nigeria, parties may not possess the same organizational and programmatic characteristics as their namesakes in more highly developed countries. According to the Nigerian definition of political parties—political action groups recognized under the laws of that country—there appears to be a plethora of such groups, particularly at the regional and lower administrative levels. However, if one were to consider only those that have contested federal elections, leaving out splinter groups or groupings temporarily created to fit a given local situation, only three may be evaluated as being of reasonably sustained consequence. The Northern People's Congress (NPC), the National Council of Nigeria and the Cameroons (NCNC), and the Action Group (AG).* The fourth, the Northern Elements Progressive Union-Sawaba (NEPU), a close ally of the NCNC, is, by all appearances, no more than an adjunct of its southern "big brother."

Subjected to the test of functional value, none of the Nigerian parties seems to possess the qualities required for high stability performance. Aside from boastful claims disseminated for publicity and propaganda purposes, none of the major parties had developed an effective machinery for interest representation in its own structure. Although their respective "images" appeared to have wider appeal, the interest politics pursued by their respective leaders were elitist to a high degree and appealed only to exceedingly small minorities, primarily among the rulers or ruling elements in the several regions and subregions. None has a following sufficient to support its claim to representativeness. The multitude of so-called party members and followers do not participate in the political process, but are bystanders, marginal to the political processes, or political subjects. Lerner inquires: "How can these modernizing societies-in-a-hurry maintain stability while rapidly acquiring mobility? In lands where people have opinions before they have jobs and cash and literacy—in short, before they have a stake in the society's efficient operation—whence will come the compulsion toward responsible formation and expression of opinion on which a free participant society depends?" [1] One might add: Whence will come a sense of stability and of continuity?

Generally, for purposes of ascertaining the stability indices in the political party sector, one might select the following factors: How many persons are materially and constantly involved in the functional aspects of political party life? How many are conscious of their activity and membership or of their association or identity

* Since January, 1962, the National Council of Nigerian Citizens.

as party members or sympathizers? And how many can articulate and/or act in one or the other of these capacities? What is the organizational depth and extent of the party? What are the major issues to which the party addresses itself and what is the relevance of these to social and political stability? What kind of leadership can be found in the party? What methods of goal realization does the leadership envisage, *privately as well as publicly?* How and by what means do the leaders expect to attain power? What is their concept of the representative processes? What is their evaluation of the goals derived from a general consensus, artificial and unrepresentative as that may be?

The bases of political parties are primarily tribal and tribal-regional. Nationalist and purely service functions contribute to their growth. Economic and social bases have not yet developed in the south to the point where political-party formation along these lines is indicated, although attempts are made on a continuing basis to bring into existence parties of that type. The Action Group in the Western Region and the National Council of Nigeria and the Cameroons are both tribal in origin and according to their principal sources of strength, and regular and reliable support—to the extent to which such is possible—appear to remain so oriented. The Northern People's Congress also is tribal-regional, although it was brought into being primarily to preserve not ethnic but economic and social interests. Its main support, however, comes from the Hausa-Fulani and northern Islamic elements. Smaller parties are either expressions of electoral expediency, reflections of personal rivalries, minorities of purely local and limited import, adherents of dynamic but isolated personalities, or temporary pressure and interest groups.

All major political parties functioning in Nigeria at the time independence was achieved had been formed, according to outward manifestations, at least, around issues related to the "struggle" for independence. In realistic political terms, they related to the struggle for control of the sources of political power and to conflicts over tribal and regional issues sometimes indirectly related to the independence problem complex. As long as there remained any uncertainty about the intentions of the colonial power, the major political parties, especially those operating in the south, had a valid rationale of wide popular appeal. Once the independence-anticolonialism issues had lost their validity, the nominal political party rationale had to shift to new grounds. Now construction of a viable, prosperous, and advanced Nigeria became the major declared focus. But all major parties had become regionally entrenched, the Action Group in the Western Region, the Northern People's Congress in the north, and the NCNC in the east. Upon the attainment of independence, they now had to defend their regional sources, which were the main bases for the continued exercise of power. All became defenders of the status quo as represented by the leadership groups in each of the regional capitals. All became, for the time being, at least, and to varying degrees, defenders of the precarious federal balance of power created by the colonial power in cooperation with some of their leaders. Therein lies one of the prime instability factors.

As has been suggested earlier—and all appearances and public utterances to the contrary notwithstanding—there is among the leading parties in Nigeria no real consensus of opinion concerning the arena within which the political struggle is to be conducted in accordance with prearranged rules. Attachment to federalist principles is a matter of political expediency, and each party aspires to become the majority party at the center at the expense of the other two major rivals. Because the leadership groups in each basically represent diametrically opposed interests, such aspirations—in themselves normally not of fundamental import and not necessarily destructive—tend to have serious unstabilizing potentialities. In the plans of each of the major parties for rule at the center, there is no room for the other two; the others are to be extinguished.

The thin veneer of agreement on fundamentals, as expressed at formal functions and ceremonials, is torn asunder as new goals and aspirations emerge. The once common opposition to colonial rule—never very much of a bond between north and south, anyway—ceases to be a valid factor in party politics upon transfer of formal political power. Now the absence of positive and constructive programs for the entire country becomes evident in all its starkness. Now the vagueness and relative meaninglessness of slogans about independence and freedom become more evident. As the gray day of post-independence responsibility dawns, the tribalist core of the parties emerges, more pronounced in its inadequacy, and the possibility of a consensus on fundamentals becomes more remote than ever. One serious weakness, then, in the political-party sector of the group complex lies in the absence of adequate correlation between the party structures and party purposes on the one hand, and the essential foci of the power struggle in the federation generally, on the other. Although the NPC came into existence primarily to give formal party expression and recognition to the informal but real power structure in the Northern Region, it has no answer to the same problems at the federal level. It is doubtful that the AG is any better prepared. Only the NCNC, with its nominally broad Pan-Africanist orientation and its apparent mass appeal, may be said to possess the capability of correlating its own activities and purposes with those relevant to the essence of power politics in Nigeria. If it is not the NCNC, then it will be a party very similar to it that will fill the present vacuum. While the NCNC is trapped, in coalition with the feudal rulers of the north, and is prevented from unfolding its revolutionary potential, the Action Group, at the federal level, seeks to assume the vacated role of champion of the downtrodden, of socialist principles, and of Pan-Africanism. It is not likely, however, that the present strategy will bring the AG to power at the federal center, for few of the programmatic points advanced by Chief Awolowo and others in the federal parliament, and in the AG-controlled press, are being applied in practice in the Western Region, where the AG has been in power for years. In terms of over-all political stability, the failure of the parties to become full-fledged supporters of a federal concept of state and society that would not only have survival value to the federation but represent social value to substantial segments of the masses in all regions spells one of the gravest elements of uncertainty.

Two of the three major parties, the NPC and the AG, came into existence partly in response to the threat of the NCNC, a mass party, to seize power nationally in behalf of a tribal group, the Ibos. The AG was the Yoruba response to the threat; the NPC, the response of the Hausa-Fulani groups and of the northern emirs. The original *raison d'être* for these parties is passé. Normally this need not be a severe handicap, but in a rapidly changing society it is. Normally, parties can disintegrate without substantially affecting the stability of the state within which they function. In the cases of the Northern and Western Regions, where the parties are identified with the ruling elements, where, in fact, it might be argued that the regions are the parties and vice versa, their disintegration would have serious effects. Through a great variety of devices, mainly directed at regional issues, the three parties have corralled, intimidated, and corrupted the voters and their local leaders in the respective regions. This has created what is essentially a regional following of sorts, but one without real social or other substance. As the importance of the region—and thereby of the major ethnic groups upon which these parties feed—diminishes in the federation, the ability of these parties to acquire strength by the accustomed means is correspondingly reduced. New issues will develop, new power patterns will emerge, and entirely new party patterns will have to be designed by those intent upon gaining a share of the power machinery. Because methods of membership and general voting recruitment have been inadequately related to the real temper and preferences of the masses during the formative stages of the prevailing system, a more accurate expression of the real, and heretofore suppressed, aspirations of the Nigerian masses will become the fulcrum of new party activity—unless a one-party dictatorship is introduced before this happens. Thus, yet another instability factor inherent in the political-party system as it operated at independence is the failure or inability of the system, and of the parties individually, to devise adequate methods of consensus measurement and to base their power on real, rather than artificial, consensus, provided of course that a consensus can be reached.

In some Nigerian circles, the thesis has been advanced that one essential ingredient of stability in the federation is the operation of a balance-of-power pattern involving the three political parties, the NPC, the AG, and the NCNC. As has been suggested earlier, this argument rests on the erroneous assumption that it is in the permanent interest of such parties to maintain the balance. Certainly, the NPC must strive to dominate and to forestall reforms at the center that might corrode the power of the emirs. The NCNC, with its claim to representation of nationalist goals, even Pan-African ones, must strive to overcome the ability of the other two to keep it from achieving its national hegemony. The will of the federalists, those who aim for greater concentration of power at the center, is going to be frustrated by the political arm of the northern emirs, who control not only the Northern Region but also the federal government by virtue of their numerical superiority in the federal parliament. Since social-economic conditions are not static, here or anywhere else, the NPC cannot forever bank on the permanent operation of the balance of power that permitted it to wield power at the federal center following the 1959 election. It must either find new allies or adjust to the changing demands of the people of Nigeria. There is no indication that this party is capable of effecting the changes demanded by an advancing society. Its interest in the preservation of the political and social status quo runs counter to the general development indicated everywhere as the destiny of Africa. On this, and on other rocks, will the balance of power founder.

One of the most severe handicaps restricting the NPC at the federal level stems from the fact that its very existence as a party was made possible only by conditions traceable to direct intervention by the colonial power. Its dominance at the federal level is the direct result of legal, administrative, and political measures taken by the colonial regime to favor the emergence of a group of

rulers based on traditional rather than modern concepts and institutions. As has been pointed out above, the very construction of
the Northern Region, in the form in which it entered the era of independence, represents one of the greatest acts of gerrymandering
in history.

It is of course possible that out of the cocoon spun in colonial
days a beautiful butterfly will ultimately emerge, for the north is
not altogether barren. It has the capability of producing new
leadership, progressive, enlightened, and secularized. Mallam
Aminu Kano, elected to the federal House of Representatives in
1959, is an example. Sir Abubakar Balewa, certainly while he was
a member of the northern House of Assembly, expressed forthright
reformist views. Even among the emirs and their immediate associates, and within northern officialdom generally, a few persons of
great promise can be identified. At the moment, however, they are
prevented by circumstances from fully unfolding their talents. But
if a progressive, enlightened group emerges, possibly as a result of
a revolt of "young Turks," one will be dealing with a new political
phenomenon. The possibility of greater proliferation in the political spectrum should not be underestimated. Through the power
of patronage, and through legal-administrative devices developed
by the colonial administration, the major parties have been able to
control the birth of rivals in their respective regions. The shortage
of leadership material also has contributed to the difficulties encountered by rival groups in attaining both political-party status
and representation at the regional or federal levels. Both the patronage and the leadership factors will diminish. As the economy
advances, other independent sources of power and influence are
created, possibly enough to facilitate the growth of effective rivals
to the major parties. Likewise, as improved educational programs
produce greater numbers of potential leaders, contestants on the
political scene will be able to survive because of improved leadership materials at their disposal. The NEPU in the north, for instance, although its chances were reduced on other accounts,
lacked effective leadership to lend support to Aminu Kano. For

support, it had to rely on the more powerful, better equipped NCNC. Likewise, the rebellious northern United Middle Belt Congress (UMBC) was similarly afflicted and had to draw, for leadership material, on the Action Group at a critical time in its existence.*

Another source of instability in the party sector derives from the weakness discussed by Lipset with reference to the integrative aspects of electoral behavior. He notes: "A stable democracy requires a situation in which all the major political parties include supporters from many segments of the population."[2] The NPC is, by and large, the party of one social division, the uppermost one in that region. The integrative aspects of the electoral processes cannot as yet unfold in that region. In the Western Region, the Action Group purports, through its extraordinary organizational skills, to give the appearance of cross-social divisional support; but it is doubtful that the lower social classes, even though they, too, may be tribally committed, consider themselves really represented by that party. Of all parties operating in Nigeria at independence, the NCNC alone appears to have possessed the potential of a mass party with substantial inter-regional and socially integrative appeal. To become fully effective, however, it would first have to divest itself of the tribalist Ibo taint, partly by broadening the base from which its leadership is drawn, partly by making concessions to other tribal and regional interests. In the future, it also will have to penetrate more successfully the social and legal roadblocks set up against its national growth, not only by the colonial regime but by the regional regimes in the north and west.

Ancient Fears, Modern Pressures

In Nigeria a larger number of nonparty groups than in more advanced societies seem to cling to the major political parties or appear to drift toward them. This seems to be so primarily because

* The UMBC grew out of the situation described in the section on ethnic minorities. It sought the creation of a separate state based on the southern portions of the Northern Region.

the major parties so decisively dominate all activities in the several regions; most associations and clubs, tribal or otherwise, address themselves to social and economic objectives within the jurisdiction of the regional governments. A few, such as the Ibo State Union, the western *Egbe Omo Oduduwa,* and several of the Islamic groups, may, in fact, represent effective centers within the NCNC, the AG, and the NPC, respectively.

The social patterns of Nigeria, with respect to group action, possess substantial tensile strength. Whatever the individual lacked in traditional society, he did not lack group association, a focus for his loyalty. In their primeval state, tribal groups possess highly integrating performance value; they act as stabilizers. If preserved in a socially feasible manner—and if one assumes that this is politically possible—tribal groups and derivative associations in the cities could serve as integrators where electoral and other modern processes must fail. With regard to the social qualities of groups of that kind, the Economic Report of 1955 noted: "Nigerians are closely tied to their immediate family or clan, they support local 'unions' [clubs], and they take pride in local achievements [the town associations]. The banding together of families, clans, and village communities of the Yorubas, and the thrift societies of the Ibo 'strangers' in the north, are practical and promising illustrations of self-help." [3]

The major source of difficulties confronting the multiple groups serving Nigerians in one form or another and for one purpose or another lies in what Lasswell refers to as the "obsolescence processes of political life." [4] As the society as a whole moves toward new frontiers and new goals, new expectations arise, and, correspondingly, the ability of given groups, organizations, and associations to assist their members toward individual goals diminishes. As the inability to perform adequately in the interest of the majority of group members is reduced, as it appears to become ever more difficult to "get results," members leave the old organizations, join new ones, or turn exclusively to their own individual devices. Where the groups remain substantially the same, in organizational-structural respects, and where the membership does not diminish substantially, the social fluidity of society in general may still radically alter the direction of the group. Thus, what by all appearances may seem to be a tribal group may already have been altered to an economic pressure group, to cite but one aspect of the problem. Likewise, groups, associations, and the like, which at one time may have had limited, local-interest focus, through association with political movements such as the Action Group, find themselves tied to regional and even national activities and concerns, and consequently undergo a thorough reorientation of goals, purposes, and, ultimately, functions as well.

Whether or not tribes have become or are becoming dysfunctional, whether or not they are losing their social and functional value, Nigeria will for some time to come be confronted by the effects of tribal politics, particularly of the politics of tribal minorities. It may well be that the *combination* of tribal disintegration and minority politics tends to unsettle so much of Nigeria's politics.

As has been noted elsewhere, Lord Hailey has described Nigeria as "perhaps the most artificial of the many administrative units created in the course of the European occupation of Africa."[5] He was, of course, referring to the ethnic factor: According to some authorities, Nigeria has more than 300 different language groups, or, if one restricts the analysis to the largest tribal groups, eleven or twelve major ones. He referred not only to the numerical proliferation of tribes, but, more important, to the decided structural and cultural divergences among them. What in some respects tends to support the decision of the colonial authorities to set up self-governing regional structures to operate within a federal structure becomes, in other respects, a source of friction, a negative force of disequilibrium and disintegration. Within each of the three regions, and within lesser administrative subdivisions, ethnic minorities fear for their survival.

The ethnic problems facing Nigeria are further compounded by religious diversity and by the developmental gap between the

north and the south, the latter roughly corresponding to the Moslem–non-Moslem distribution that finds the Moslem population
predominantly in the less developed north or interior. The resultant political frictions and pressures are accentuated by the events
preceding and following independence. Each minority group—
that is, each ethnic or religious group that, by administrative acci-
dent or by intent, has been assigned to an unfriendly, even hostile
majority—fears that a transfer of power from relatively sympathetic and comparatively neutral British hands to the rulers of
"hereditary or traditional enemies," or to nonbelievers, will cause a
chain of events that will ultimately lead to the total destruction
of the group.[6]

Major Ethnic Minority Groups

1. Western Region (predominantly Yoruba: 4.3 million)

Fears

Edo-speaking	446,000	a. Yoruba domination
Urhobo	243,000	b. Use of regional coercive apparatus against
Ibo	250,000	minorities
Ijaw	65,000	c. Economic discrimination
Itsekirri	21,000	d. Under-representation in parliamentary
		bodies
		e. Fraudulent election procedures
		f. Administrative oppression
		g. Discrimination in administration of local
		government
		h. Discrimination in public services—educa-
		tion, teaching of Arabic to Moslems, etc.

2. Northern Region (predominantly Hausa-Fulani: 8.5 million)

Fears

Kanuri	1,175,000	a. After independence the more conservative
Nupe	347,000	tendencies of the "northern system" will
Yoruba	536,000	prevail against minorities
Tiv	772,000	b. Moves toward democracy will be aban-
Others	c. 5,000,000	doned
		c. Tolerance toward non-Moslems will be
		abandoned
		d. Neglect of minority areas for public serv-
		ices—hospitals, roads, schools
		e. Preferential treatment accorded to Islam
		and Hausa language
		f. Reduction in importance of traditional

Major Ethnic Minority Groups (continued)

leaders of minority groups against emirs and their appointees

g. Imposition of Moslem rules concerning political role of women on all other groups

h. Lack of impartiality on the part of the judicial and police apparatus

i. Administrative discrimination and favoritism for majority party

j. Fears regarding influence of Arabic north —U.A.R.

k. Administrative and political discrimination against non-Islamic local government

l. The threat of Moslem law generally.

3. Eastern Region (predominantly Ibo: 5 million)

Fears

Ijaw	250,000	a. Political domination by Ibos (NCNC)
Efik	71,000	b. Autocracy or dictatorship (Zikism)
Ibibio	747,000	c. Packing of public posts and services with Ibos
		d. Bypassing and reduction in importance of local government and chiefs
		e. Manipulation of legal system in favor of Ibos; administrative discrimination
		f. Operation of "strong-arm" groups (Zikist National Vanguard)

SOURCES: Great Britain, *Cmnd.* 505 (1958); Coleman, *op. cit.*, p. 15.

Although the three major groups, the Hausa-Fulani, the Ibo, and the Yoruba, present the principal sources of conflict based on ethnic considerations, there is no reason to doubt that any of the smaller units, if given political power over other lesser minorities, will not also produce similarly structured conflict situations. However, for present purposes, the north-west-east triangle should suffice as a frame for discussion. Of the three groups, the Yoruba have developed the most organized approach to ethnocentrism in their political conduct. The Yoruba-Western political party, the Action Group's main carrier of the ethnic cause, has already been referred to—the ethnically-culturally oriented *Egbe Omo Oduduwa*. There is little doubt that the Action Group aspires toward the concentration of all Yoruba or predominantly Yoruba minority sections in the north and east into a single Yoruba region or state.

The Action Group's electoral effort in all three regions during the 1959 pre-independence campaign was based partly on the theme of Yoruba unification and partly on the exploitation of non-Yoruba minority fears in the north and east. Considerable sums of money were applied toward the expansion of the Action Group from a purely regional to a national party. The results indicate that the appeal was successful mainly in the Western Region itself; outside the region, it succeeded wherever non-Yoruba minorities required outside support against the Hausa-Fulani, the Ibo, or other groups of actual or imagined hostile intent. The appeal of the AG outside the Western Region wisely refrained from identifying local minority aspirations with those of the Yoruba group; instead, AG propaganda focused on local grievances of an economic, administrative, legal, or cultural nature. In so doing, AG propaganda tended to accentuate ethnic claims and conflicts that might otherwise have been mitigated or at least remained dormant. Nearly every argument in favor of these non-western groups—the Tiv and Jukun of the Benue plains, small groups in the Cameroon mountains, and the Ibibio and Efik of the eastern and coastal regions—was applied in turn by the NPC, the NCNC, and others against the Yoruba in the Western Region and in support of ethnic argumentation there.

The nation-wide appeal of the NCNC was slightly more successful than the AG attempt in creating a national image. Even so, NCNC candidates were elected primarily on ethnic grounds in areas outside its own base, the Eastern Region. The conclusion seems to be warranted that the 1959 elections to the federal House of Representatives underlined the fact that each region consists of two areas: a core area, with a high degree of ethnic homogeneity and tribal resilience and a relatively high level of economic and cultural development; and a peripheral area, where many lesser tribes live on a lower level of economic development. The core areas are subjected to an ever-increasing concentration by regional authorities on the perpetuation and further development of ethnic characteristics. The full weight of the Northern Regional

Government, spiritual and secular, with its nearly total control of all aspects of life there, is being applied to the strengthening of the Hausa-Fulani Islamic rule. The machinery of the Eastern Region works toward the entrenchment of Ibo rule there and the extension of Ibo influence through the agencies of the NCNC and the Ibo National Union, an extremely well-organized and effective ethnic-political unit with branches wherever a significant number of Ibos reside. The spirit of the *Egbe Omo Oduduwa* permeates the Western Region and beyond, wherever Yorubas are found. Smaller ethnic units find it increasingly difficult to carry out their own ethnification efforts. The 1959 election results, while confirming the existence of strong ethnic centers in all three regions, also confirmed the conclusion of the 1958 Minorities Commission that many of the smaller tribes lack the requisite cohesion to qualify for separate administrative treatment.

With the aid of the colonial power, which retains an interest in the survival of a federation so laboriously constructed, a number of steps have been taken to reinforce the structure and to generate stabilizing influences in the ethnic and religious conflicts. First, there are, of course, the efforts to create a Nigerian symbolism to which all conflicting groups can subscribe. The first stanza of the national anthem adopted at the time of independence, primarily for the celebrations, illustrates the problem graphically:

> Nigeria, we hail thee
> Our own dear native land
> Though tribe and tongue may differ
> In Brotherhood we stand,
> Nigerians all and proud to serve
> Our sovereign Motherland.*

The combined operations of all federal services and industrial enterprises are attempting further to solidify the image of a Nigerian nation before it has acquired legal-political substance.[7]

---

* At the time of adoption, the first stanza, in particular, was criticized not only because the entire anthem had been written by a British national, but because the reference to tribal diversity was not in the best interest of promotion of a Nigerian theme.

The legal-administrative steps taken to ameliorate the minority group problem in favor of greater stability are in themselves indicative of the gravity of the situation. In the main, these measures seem to be addressed to relatively insignificant aspects of the conflicts, although some surely have immediate or potential stabilizing value. In theory, the establishment of a federal system of government should constitute a most significant step—through provisions for a legal-administrative machinery to resolve conflicts along ethnic lines—toward the stabilization of polities. However, there is room for suspicion that the division into three regions roughly coinciding with tribal core areas—Hausa-Fulani, Yoruba, and Ibo—was motivated, in part, by a desire to perpetuate rather than to resolve, ethnic conflicts. The 1958 enquiry into the grievances of minority groups was partly traceable to these suspicions, most strongly held in "Zikist" circles.

The report of the Minorities Commission and the several constitutional conferences preceding and following it brought into sharp focus the needs of the country for machinery that would resolve this type of conflict, and the legal-administrative framework, which was incorporated into the federal and regional constitutions, reflected the general conviction that Nigeria's continued existence as a viable state depended on the continued recognition of ethnic grievances and the creation of machinery to solve the conflicts on a mutually agreeable basis.[8] The following represents the extent of the major formal legal-administrative conciliation measures incorporated in the pre-independence constitutional documents:

1. Creation of a bicameral federal legislature
2. Incorporation of comprehensive provisions safeguarding human rights, based mainly on the Convention for the Protection of Human Rights and Fundamental Freedoms
3. Provision for entrenched clauses concerning constitutional amendment
4. Federal control over the police, with regional representation on the controlling Council, including the absorption of local forces into the federal force

5. Uniformity concerning electoral provisions
6. Strengthening of federal supervision over judicial administration, coupled with reform of regional systems
7. Regional reforms and adjustments in accordance with the recommendations of the Minorities Commission
8. Central control of prisons
9. Strengthening of the position of chiefs
10. Creation of "minority areas" where necessary[9]

At the regional level, these recommendations led to a number of reforms in anticipation of independence. The fears of the non-Islamic minorities in the north were recognized, at least formally, in the Penal Code Law of 1959, referred to earlier. Reforms under this code were patterned after the legal systems in other countries where Moslems and non-Moslems live side by side—for example, Lybia, Sudan, and Pakistan. The principal point of reform was the introduction of a codified system of criminal law enforceable in all courts, instead of being enforceable only in either Moslem or non-Moslem courts and thus productive of injustice where jurisdiction could not be objectively determined. Moslem law as such was confined to the law of personal status and family relations and to civil cases in certain instances. Other reforms sought to transfer control over the native courts from local authority, the emirs, to the region.[10]

All regions have attempted to reform, where necessary, the system of appointment and removal of chiefs in anticipation of the creation of the federal House of Chiefs and in response to demands by minorities that their traditional leaders not be discriminated against within the several regions.[11]

It goes without further emphasis that, in purely administrative respects, only time and the confluence of nonadministrative factors will produce the attitudes and procedures requisite for effective and lasting resolution of conflicts on ethnic grounds. The Penal Code in the north, for instance, will for some time to come be ignored wherever emirs and *alkalai* are confident that they are relatively unobserved and beyond immediate political challenge.

Politics is a continual process of compromise between what is desired and what is possible and—looking at the situation in the broad-
est terms—it seems that for some time to come compromise at the
center will be forced on each of the regions. It is on this argument
that hopes must rest, both of the continued unity of Nigeria and of
justice for individuals. In each region there is a majority group which
seems likely to hold together and which might impose its will in its
own interests on the minority if the region were entirely isolated. But
since each of these majority groups forms the nucleus of a national
party, and each needs all the support it can get in the federal elections, each will have to seek the favor of the minorities.[12]

The political processes generally, and the operations of the
several political parties particularly, are bound to serve as conciliation machinery in the informal realm of real, practical politics. In the course of national electioneering, what would otherwise be regional or parochial parties must now assume national
posture. National images are produced to fit party-political objectives. Dependencies, in the party-political sense, are created
across regional and ethnic boundaries through the transfer of
funds and the allocation of public and private patronage in recognition of party-political services. As the NCNC, AG, and the
Northern People's Congress (which considers renaming itself the
Nigerian People's Party) extend their operations across the Nigerian political landscape in quest of a working majority at the
federal level, multiple ethnic divisions are crossed and obliterated
in terms of personal loyalties. The Ibo-dominated NCNC's alliance with the Islamic Northern Elements Progressive Union
is bound to reduce the culture gap between progressive northern
Moslems and progressive southern non-Moslems. It is possible that
the operations of the Yoruba-dominated AG in the Northern and
Eastern Regions also creates zones of ethnic indifference.

Both regional elections for houses of assembly and federal elections for the House of Representatives, over a period of time, will
clarify the relative position of given ethnic minorities in each
region. In elections, parties generally appeal vigorously to ethnic
survival interests and prejudices, especially in the so-called mi-

nority areas: Ilorin-Kabba, Niger Delta, Calabar, and Middle-Belt. Inasmuch as most, but not all, administrative boundaries were drawn with ethnic divisions in mind, entire blocs of federal electoral districts (constituencies) may be considered expressive of ethnic interests wherever the districts lie entirely within given administrative subdivisions.[13]

Numerous political conflicts based on ethnic divergencies take place at the municipal or district level. Although these do not necessarily affect the ethnic balance in the country as a whole, the sum of such conflicts must necessarily be taken into account in a discussion of political stability in the federation. For it is at the local level frequently that amalgamation and integration can politically best be effected. Personal mobility, relative sophistication, high concentration of transpersonal relations through churches, functional associations, etc. are likely to create communities of interest transcending ethnic divisions. And in view of the fact that the centers of gravity of Nigerian politics are found in urban population concentrations, the local and municipal scene cannot be overlooked.

Communal conflict, however, is a constant feature of towns in which ethnic units are geographically divided. Where this is the case, political-party and factional operations tend to accentuate ethnic division. The *sabon garis* of cities like Kano, for instance, are distasteful from the Hausa-Fulani point of view. Since they have heavy Ibo and Yoruba concentrations, they are citadels of the Ibo National Union, the NCNC, and the AG, all of which are revolutionary in terms of the prevailing Islamic order.[14]

Where urban centers include heavy concentrations of "strangers" with a relatively high degree of expectation in terms of improved living standards, public services, etc., political conflict is inevitable. Many, if not all, of the conflicts encountered in the urban centers of Nigeria, such as Lagos, Ibadan, and Port Harcourt, are ethnic in nature and are traceable to economic discontent of minority groups concentrated in these cities.[15]

The foregoing indicates that implicit in the legal-political structure is the machinery for the effective reduction, if not resolution, of conflicts based on ethnic diversity. If for a reasonable period of time conditions permit the diversion of popular attention from the ancient and entrenched fears and grievances, countervailing forces will probably reduce the problems of tribalism to minor proportions, primarily because tribes are rapidly losing both their rationale for existence and their utility value. On the other hand, failure elsewhere in state and society may bring either a regression or, where tensions already are high, an accentuation of these fears and grievances to the point where a solution may be out of reach.

Trade Unions

At independence, Nigerian trade unions were too weak to act either as stabilizing or as revolutionary agents. Prior to independence, the political goals posed by the so-called anticolonial or anti-imperialist struggle had galvanizing effects upon some trade unions, but post-independence labor goals were quite different. In order for trade unionism to retain the interest and allegiance of its members and to strengthen itself nationally, it had to develop a positive, constructive, and economically realistic program. But Nigerian trade unionism was almost totally lacking in the talent, the experience, and the know-how necessary to live up to the new requirements. It lacked, and still does lack, an ideological foundation. Unlike similar organizations in French territories, which benefited by a close association with metropolitan France, Nigeria's labor movement, if it can be described as one, developed in all essential respects as an orphan, notwithstanding occasional exploratory visits by trade-union representatives from Britain and the United States. The movement lacked social and economic direction: Strikes were erratic, irrational, and more often than not over the wrong issues at the wrong time; tribalism raised havoc with organizational goals, a fact which was exploited successfully by management.

Furthermore, the workers were too few and too scattered to be able to play a significant role either for or against the stability of the new federation.[16] The principal weapon, the strike, was also ineffectual because, at best, it had only nuisance value. A general strike, for instance, would affect only the relatively small business and industrial interests; it would not affect the preponderantly agricultural pursuits that will be the lifeblood of the nation for some time to come. The stoppage of postal communications, while extremely annoying to the government and the commercial interests, would hardly faze the general population. It would merely amount to temporary loss of what in Nigeria is still a luxury, for the ordinary man outside the metropolitan centers has enough food for himself and for his family and would, therefore, not be overly concerned about a stoppage of food delivery. In the relatively few places where such stoppage could provoke a serious crisis, the armed forces and the police could effectively counter the effects. Furthermore, unions have not yet accumulated sufficient funds to sustain a strike of any length; under prevailing conditions, they would not stand a chance against determined efforts by government or management to bring them to their knees. The Nigerian economy, for some time to come, will not be a wage economy, and trade unionism, unless utilized for auxiliary political purposes, as has been the case in Ghana, will remain a marginal force.

While it must be conceded that the germ of trade unionism was deliberately planted in Nigeria by emissaries of the British Labour Party and the Trade Union Council, it also must be noted that the "push" from London was countered by the "pull" in Lagos, Enugu, Ibadan, and Kaduna. The colonial administration and the expatriate economic forces on the local scene managed to contain the growth of a Nigerian trade-union movement. In so doing, they failed to prepare Nigerian labor for a constructive role in a modern democracy. If Nigerian unionism is presently incapable of performing in an integrative fashion, if it should become dysfunctional to democratic forms or stability in general, the responsibility will rest, to a large extent, with the European colonial regime whose trade-union legislation has been described as a "guideline to anarchy."[17] It appears that atomization rather than integration was the objective of the trade-union policy of the European rulers and, incidentally, of their Nigerian partners also.[18]

Although the Nigerian economy does not as yet favor a strong, massive trade-union movement, relatively weak movements elsewhere in Africa have spawned competent, responsible leadership, which has enjoyed direct links to the masses and thus has commanded their confidence.

Nothwithstanding the relatively large number of members claimed by the regional and national unions, the movement is still in its infancy. It has been harassed, where not bribed or bought, and its leaders have at times been hounded into submission through the use of blacklists or shifted from positions of influence and prestige through administrative arrangements. Therefore it appears that the greatest element of instability in the trade-union movement, especially the individual groups composing it, has been the failure to integrate it, or, at least, its key groups, in the political structure and system. Already there are signs that frustration among workers leads to a search for effective alternatives to legitimate trade-union activity. The preferences of the younger, more impatient leaders indicate an increased orientation toward revolutionary goals and an interest in the establishment of ties to the Communist bloc.

Secret Societies

The rules concerning the obsolescence processes of political life, stated by Lasswell, should be especially relevant to the tribal secret societies. Traditionally, these societies performed what may be described as the secret police and policy functions within the tribal unit. Surrounded by secret ritual, including masked dances with calculated terroristic impact, some of them represented a constructive functional aspect of traditional society. They were instrumental in the maintenance of law and order and the upkeep of moral standards. Some, of course, used their power for their own ends, such as the Leopard Society among the Ibo and a few lesser, more ephemeral ones in eastern Nigeria. From the point of view of this study, secret societies generally should be regarded as rather inconsequential. Their ability to influence in any material way the significant aspects of political-power processes is waning as modern police organization improves and extends its scope into all areas. Education, improved communications, and general social mobility tend to reduce both the utility value and the political, coercive potency of secret societies to the vanishing point. However, as occurred in Kenya, the Cameroons, and elsewhere, such groups may, under certain conditions, experience a rebirth. Frustrations among displaced and socially discarded tribal functionaries, especially those whose function it had been to manipulate the tribal symbol toward traditional social and political goals, could strengthen or recreate the secret societies, or create new ones. The major purpose would be similar to that served by associations such as the Black Hand or the Mafia in certain parts of the Western world, and the role of witchcraft in postmedieval Europe may also be analogous.

In the Moslem areas, groups such as the *Tijaniyya* and *Qadiriyya,* although at times functioning in the fashion of secret organizations, may not be classified as such. They are mentioned only because they may, under certain conditions, lend themselves to secretive purposes. Since, as pointed out above, these groups pursue missionary objectives aimed at a return to Islamic orthodoxy, reactionary and regressive elements in the north may wish to make use of groups of that kind to circumvent both the overtly political organizations and the secular structure in general.

Dark Horses

Political analysis would be incomplete if it were to disregard those forces that at the moment of analysis have not yet assumed recognizable forms. In his chapter on "The New Towns," Hodgkin sketches some of these forces.[19] The prime stimulants to life in the new town are the processes and consequences of urbanization. Here a new elite develops, sophisticated, rootless, free thinking, and rebellious, and here women assume independent roles. Young men assume the prime prestige and power positions, through either legitimate or illicit activities, through either honest professional pursuit or crime. Here Westernization, perhaps also Easternization, sets in. Thus, we may generalize that the political stability of the new state will certainly be affected by the forces gathering momentum in the new towns, in Lagos, in the new quarters of Ibadan, in Enugu, etc. It is from these germinating centers of activity that new ideas, especially secular ideas, will spring; from there, new assaults upon the old order will not only be engineered, but may, in fact, be executed through channels leading directly to political-party, governmental, and administrative headquarters. It may well be that the most effective challenge to the northern rulers, temporarily entrenched at the federal center, will emanate not from known organizations but from the unorganized but exceedingly potent elements forming in the towns. Already, the Lagosian, the inhabitant of the enclave that serves as the federal capital, constitutes a breed quite distinct from any other in Nigeria.

The developmental problems confronting the administrations of the growing municipalities, the result of the concentrated impact on large segments of the population, contain the potentialities of instability. The rapid growth of the urban centers outstrips available housing and authorities are unable to provide the necessary services, let alone find the means of constructing adequate homes.[20] These and other problems, which are growing into massive proportions because of the numbers involved and outweigh, politically, the problems of the rural population, are likely to affect the social and political system far more drastically than could be expected of any of the existing organized forces. Hodgkin writes: "The new towns generate a social life of their own—

unlike any life that has existed in Africa hitherto: deriving its special qualities, first, from the new emphasis upon money and consumption; second, from the search for liberty; and third, from the influence of the European world and its value."[21] Now there should be added the ferment that originates in the Communist part of the world.

Not to be overlooked in that connection, primarily because of its concentration in the cities, is the new class of people working for government in one capacity or another.[22] Together with their counterparts in industry, commerce, and the social services, they represent a force that, if combined for common goals, could be superior to any other in terms of concentration of education, technical skills, and proximity to sources of action, political thought, and both the communication channels and the political-strategic command posts in general.

The promotion of new ideas and of new social, cultural, and political concepts by government employees is, of course, far more evident in the south than in the relatively well-controlled and regulated north. But the northern brand of reformer, though docile and conformist for the moment, should not be underestimated. The recent reforms of the Northern Regional Penal Code, and other changes and improvements, may gradually reduce the control capabilities of the ruling element there and strengthen the forces intent on challenging feudalism and tradition. Still, as a group, the challenging forces are inarticulate, for the career opportunities outside the confines of the established order are virtually nonexistent. But the temper of these forces may be perceived through cautious inquiry on specific test subjects. When confronted by questions concerning freedom of speech, the role of women in society and polity, education and technological progress, popular democracy and its institutional and procedural implications, their preferences, hidden thoughts, and aspirations are revealed.

The political implications of the clash between Islam and Christianity also point to the emergence of new groups and forces, the stability value of which varies from north to south. Opportunities for action by these forces are derived from what may accurately be described as a fundamental incompatibility between cultural and psychological needs of the West African Negro and the prevailing forms of Christianity. Elements oriented toward Islam, or identified with it, view Christianity not only as an alien way of life, but, most important, as a source of instability that must be resisted as strongly as any other revolutionary force or doctrine. They are confident that Islam will ultimately vanquish Christianity in Africa, primarily because it is an Eastern—or, better, non-Western, religion—and it can adapt itself without special effort to the African way of life and mentality. The African, as yet culturally uncommitted, finds it much easier to conform to Islamic law and morality than to the requirements of Christianity. There is evidence of systematic efforts by the rulers of the north to exploit this tendency. The United Arab Republic, Saudi Arabia, and other north and northeast African centers, or outlets of Islamic culture, also appear to be active in that direction. It is to be expected that even the Communist states will seek to exploit this particular opportunity for anti-Western activity.

On the other hand, Christian forces, primarily the Roman Catholic Church, show signs that they would prefer not to allow the opportunity for the militant advance of their faith to pass without a struggle. As long as the northern rulers exercise as strong a hold on the federal government as they did at independence, activities of the Christian groups will be restricted, as they are in the north, to secular pursuits, such as extension of medical aid and certain types of technical training.

In passing, it should be noted that sub-Saharan Islam, as it begins to manifest itself in formerly pagan or even Christian areas in the southern coastal region, is considerably less militant than its parent in the Middle East. It is, therefore, quite possible that progressive Islamization of an area such as Nigeria, partly because Africa and Africans are not altogether passive and without inherent cultural strength and viability, will become a moderating and stabilizing force. Perhaps an African version of Islam could provide the very integrative qualities that political parties, modern social organizations, and the like do not possess and that other revolutionary forces do possess but should perhaps not be allowed to exercise in Nigeria.

7

The Way of Doing Things

Basic Functional and Procedural Aspects

No degree of institutional refinement of a social or political system will be adequate if administrative skills are nonexistent or inadequate. More generally, the functional and procedural aspects of society and polity frequently spell the difference between a well-nigh worthless piece of paper and an effective, working constitution, between disorder and stability. Many a review or so-called analysis of contemporary African states and societies lacks value because it neglects to assess adequately the functional and procedural dimensions, or more specifically, the manner in which broad principles, general propositions, and written legal provisions are translated into living social and political action. To that end, a meaningful evaluation of political stability in Nigeria necessitates a close look at the more critical strategic skills and techniques required for government and administration, as related to some of the functional and procedural aspects of the economy, of education, and of the parliamentary and political institutions.

Organizing Power

In order for political power to amount to more than temporary exercise of prerogatives, it must be organized. In Nigeria, the organization of power for the creation of political stability, whether for democratic or nondemocratic purposes, is extremely weak, and the most promising prospects are in the Western Region. This applies equally to the intellectual, administrative, and technical facets and instrumentalities required for the effective organization of power. At the time of independence, there were far too few in-

144

dividuals who possessed the competence required for the operation of a reasonably efficient governmental mechanism. Too few commanded the necessary intellectual capabilities to conceive innovations and to make adjustments or changes. Too few persons were acquainted with the social, economic, political, and cultural conditions in their own local environment, let alone those prevailing nationally, to conceive of policies and to prescribe courses of action that would have been meaningful in the Nigerian setting.

Systems of government with a preference for minimum state direction of private affairs will tend to accentuate the problem because of an absence of elements of compulsion concerning individual choices of career and vocation. The northern rulers, in several crisis situations that developed shortly before and after the attainment of independence, displayed an almost complete lack of know-how in their attempts to deal with the conditions facing them. This was not so much because of a lack of competent personnel in high positions of government, since most of the expatriate permanent secretaries then were still on the job, but because of a dearth of talent and of effective administrative instrumentalities down the line and on the spot where trouble was likely to erupt. The native authorities, upon which the northern regime relies for much of the organization of power, are progressively less and less capable of dealing with serious crises such as massive insurrection and widespread rebellion. As the probability of major disturbances increases in the north, the capability of the regime to resist and to extend its power effectively into all areas under its control diminishes correspondingly.

In the southern areas, especially in the Western Region, government can rely to a greater extent on effective instrumentalities to organize power. The political-party striking force developed by the Action Group, under brilliant leadership, serves as a good illustration. The effective political leader of that region, Chief Awolowo, and several of his lieutenants possess organizational skills equal to those marshalled by any group of leaders elsewhere.

But the question of depth cannot be answered as satisfactorily. Efficiency and reliability decrease sharply down the administrative line. In the east, the situation is even less encouraging.

Now that society in Nigeria has been opened up and a multitude of conflicting and competing forces have been released, the authoritarian regime operated by the British with such relative ease cannot as readily be emulated by Nigerians. It would be especially difficult for one single leader, or a single group, to attempt to erect, and to operate successfully, a Nigeria-wide regime with totalitarian tendencies and intents. This would be difficult not only because a substantial segment of the Nigerian population may have an aversion to totalitarian rule and methods, but because a plethora of administrative factors would bedevil such a system and would soon commit it to ineffectiveness. Moreover, under favorable conditions, the still powerful, influential, and relatively cohesive tribal-traditional forces, which are most cohesive if called upon to offer resistance to strangers or to strange ways, in all probability would serve as effective rallying points for groups favoring greater decentralization.

In any case, in order for central seizure of power and its sustained exercise by one man or by a small clique to become possible, it would be necessary, among other things, to weld together large sections of the country, partly by incisive reforms in public administration, and to create a more nationally oriented service.

Extending and Applying Power

As long as the British expatriates were exclusively in control of the administration and of the technical manipulation of the state apparatus, not much of a functional problem existed in that sector, provided one did not set the administrative and developmental standards too high. The colonial bureaucracy functioned reasonably well, since it had an adequate understanding of the wider ramifications and over-all purposes of administration. However, the sharply increasing demands placed on the administrative and technical services after independence, coupled with the transfer of control over the services from colonial to indigenous personnel, inevitably resulted in a reduction of the stability value of these services. Also, the capabilities of these services to hold together divergent sections, interests, and groups, to perform minimum functions, and, beyond that, to direct the advance of Nigerian society toward new social, economic, and political goals were materially reduced.

During the period of colonial hegemony, reasonably well-trained Westerners operated a Western system of government and administration, primarily to satisfy Western goals. These goals were rather modest by Western standards; the pace of administrative production was rather leisurely, and the opportunities for sidetracking unpleasant tasks or for burying them altogether were many. The south had few competent critics who could look over the shoulders of the British civil servants and understand what they were doing, let alone criticize them for shortcomings. The north had fewer. Besides, there were effective ways and means to remove from the scene, or render harmless, any seriously troublesome critic. The machinery of government was well shielded from African critics.

Independence tends to change this situation substantially. Now, inadequately trained Africans—with few exceptions—are to operate a system that they do not fully approve of and that they probably do not fully comprehend in its philosophic and functional ramifications. The new bureaucracy goes through the motions of administrative performance without the requisite conceptualization of the deeper, long-range procedural implications of what they are doing or of the end effects of their actions and plans. They do not adequately comprehend the social and political goals, the implications, and the social and political consequences of their actions. Too many of them understand only the immediate routine of the office to which they have been assigned, but lack a conceptualization of the over-all administrative organization of which they are a part. Again, as in all other sectors, especially the southern regions, Nigeria has brilliant exceptions. Some offices in the Western Region are models of efficiency by any standards. But the needed shock troops are too few, the front is too thin, and the problems are too many and continually mounting. A bewildering array of equally attractive but conflicting models from all parts of the world further compound the problems. Although the same amount of paperwork may be moved from office to office after independence as before, it is generally done with sharply reduced efficiency. In the east, where, for many years prior to 1960, political considerations consistently prevailed in civil-service recruitment and personnel policies, the administration is far below the level required by considerations of public safety.

As the country advances technologically, as society becomes more complex, the African administrator will find it more difficult to perform adequately in terms of minimum goals and responsibilities. The perceptions of the new personnel about the scope of their tasks, of questions of legal limitation, of jurisdiction, and of public relations will for some time to come be considerably inferior to that of the expatriates. And because the latter represented a foreign power and alien culture, they could not always be expected to be models of devotion to Nigerian needs. Given a gradual development of the country, the bureaucracy might grow to reasonably adequate proportions. But by all indications, the impact of the jet and satellite age, revolutionary improvements in all spheres of human activity, and the impact of big-power politics tend to impede the chances of orderly, systematic growth. To remain competitive externally, to remain adequate internally, both the indigenous regime and the supporting bureaucracy must exert themselves, probably well beyond the point of endurance. It is unlikely that a bureaucracy that barely controls the somewhat archaic, obsolescent machinery of government handed over by the colonial regime will find the time or inclination to study diligently the new frontiers of technology and science and to address itself to new social concepts. Much of this is, of course, reminiscent of bureaucracies elsewhere; however, pressures for new ways and improved techniques will mount more sharply in Nigeria than, let us say, in Great Britain.

Administrative skills acquired under British rule were adequate for some regional purposes, but not necessarily adequate for federal ones. Too few Nigerians had reason or opportunity to develop either administrative skills of adequate scope or the requisite concepts for foreign-policy formulation, conduct, and international cooperation. British talent had handled empire and commonwealth relations; but now, an entirely new dimension was added. To meet the demands of the new diplomatic dimension, some Nigerians had been, and still are being, trained in British embassies abroad and in London. But more is needed. There can be little doubt that Nigeria lacks the developed talent for the conduct of diplomatic relations commensurate with a nation of her size and importance. The intricacies of international trade and of international security problems are well beyond the ken of all but a handful of Nigerian personnel, although it should be noted that they possess capabilities of the highest quality. The skills required for independent existence are not there. Britain has the intention and the capability to step up assistance in the development of the needed skills, and other Western countries are willing to aid. Many Nigerians, at the moment of independence, generally appeared to be resigned to an extended period of apprenticeship under foreign tutelage. The question that looms large, however, with special reference to political stability, is whether the attitude of patience in this respect will last long enough. Where self-administration lags behind self-government—and that was the case in Nigeria in 1960—a political problem arises that only the most circumspect and skilled political leadership can regulate and contain. Massive aid and assistance from abroad, if wisely applied, could lay the foundations for a reasonably adequate, modestly advanced social edifice; but the question remains whether or not conditions will permit the foundation to harden and to settle.

Commenting on the findings and recommendations of a parliamentary committee, the Federal Government, in 1960, made the following observation:

> The Government agrees with the view of the Parliamentary Committee that Nigeria is not yet at a stage where rigid standards of quality and performance can reasonably be demanded of the Public Service. In a period of transition, a temporary deterioration must be expected and must also be tolerated if the new status of the Service is to be successfully achieved.
>
> Some loss of output and efficiency, while the new generation of Nigerian officers are gaining experience and confidence, is a loss gladly suffered with a view to future gain.
>
> As to the present state of the administrative-executive Civil Service, the Government is under no illusion. It consists of a limited number of experienced officers, expatriate and Nigerian, and a much larger number of young officers who are struggling against time to fit themselves to assume the higher responsibilities which must shortly fall to them.[1]

One element of deterioration of the public service must be traced to the Federal Government itself, in particular to the predominant Northern Region contingent in it. Insistence by northerners that the ratio of approximately fifty-fifty be applied throughout the federal service with regard to north-south representation in all superscale posts brings to a virtual halt operation in certain departments where officers of seniority but of southern origin are compelled to remain frozen in their posts while the country awaits the emergence of suitably trained northern Hausa candidates. Many of the candidates advanced by the north are, in fact, semiliterate and extremely inexperienced.[2]

Not as Taught at Oxford

Those skills that specifically involve law and justice are generally related to the administrative skills. Access to the legislative functions, to the courts, and to related agencies of the law is a key objective of political strategy in the power struggle everywhere. Likewise, the attainment of political stability in the sense in which it is used here, especially in relatively open societies, depends greatly upon the ability to devise meaningful, relevant, and effective rules, to devise agencies and develop channels for the effective administration and application of these rules, and to develop and operate effective supervisory and enforcement organs. Where these aspects of rule are neglected, or where the means for effective handling of them do not exist, the organization of power cannot proceed toward the creation of conditions of political stability.

During the colonial regime, it was established policy to permit the traditional legal systems and practices to prevail in all areas not of immediate economic-strategic value to the colonial interests. Hailey notes: "It was fortunate that in so many areas of European rule, the majority of civil issues, including those arising in the field of personal law, as also the less important criminal cases, continued to be tried by native tribunals which followed their own traditional procedure."[3] It can be generalized, then, that the retention of chiefly powers, a practice in areas not of strategic import, plus the retention of traditional judicial systems and practices, permitted the manipulation of the latter in the interest of traditional rule. To deprive the chiefs of judicial power was to reduce them to political impotence. Hailey's remark that "the chief is no chief if he has no court" summarizes the problem succinctly.[4] Legal concepts developed under conditions of identity of political and legal-judicial administration, as has been characteristic of traditional systems in all parts of Nigeria, were likely to be more political than legal. Rules developed under those conditions could always be expected to have as a prime purpose the maintenance of the established regime without allowance for change of any kind. The entire legal system, and all auxiliary functions of state and society, were intended to maintain the status quo and political stability, not in the sense in which the term is used here but in an absolute sense. Since no material change was expected, or tolerated, stability did not depend upon rules permitting change, orderly though it might be. Thus, a major problem arises for the new Nigerian state: the development of concepts of legality, of law-making, administering, and enforcement, not only for the

preservation of an arbitrarily determined status quo but for substantive change. Among other things, this requires a willingness
on the part of the wielders of effective power in the regions, as
well as at the federal level, to allow the separation of legislative,
executive, and judicial functions, at least to the extent necessary
to permit outside groups and interests not integrally part of government to make themselves felt. This will prove to be most difficult to achieve in the north.

In the north, the web of authority, at the time of independence,
was far too tight to permit an immediate alteration of the system
along these lines, in spite of nominal legal reform. It has already
been suggested that it is doubtful whether the reforms significantly affected the effective power structure there. They certainly
did not materially alter the functional concepts of the ruling group
concerning law, administration, and justice in relation to politics.
In the Western Region, the pattern of legal, judicial, and related
administrative functions differs considerably from the pattern in
the north, although the new rulers, including the chiefs identified
with the new rule, frequently appear to utilize the Customary
Courts as weapons against change in order to impair the chances
of oppositional elements to gain ground and to discipline recalcitrants in their own ranks. In the east, where the web of authority
under traditional rule had never achieved the degree of cohesiveness now prevalent there, the welding of political, legal, judicial,
and administrative functions takes on a more modern, if inefficient
and, at times, chaotic, form. In the final analysis, however, the
functional and procedural aspects of law do not differ here much
from those elsewhere.

As far as the Nigerian side is concerned, the legislative function,
and everything flowing directly from it, cannot be said to rest on
firm, functional, and historical precedence. Throughout the history of the country, the legislative function was wholly secondary
to other functions of the governmental apparatus. "In primitive conditions that which lies most in the background is the legislative power; that which is most distinctly conceived is judicial

power."[5] During the greater part of the colonial regime, the legislative branches were mere sounding boards for the Colonial Office and its representatives on the scene. The main purpose of legislation was to maintain order and to endow economic exploitation with legality. Even where legislation tended to be socially meaningful, its administration by the European service tended to negate or counteract its surface purposes. The administrative and legislative functions, evaluated together, spelled autocratic rule, and administration outweighed the legislative power through interpretation and application. It may be said that Africans studying under British permanent secretaries may well have arrived at the conclusion that the locus of power in government resides not in the legislature, not in the top cabinet offices, but in the offices of the top civil servants, where the law is provided with the requisite administrative twist—where, at times, the law originates, in effect.

Addressing himself to the Western world primarily, Lasswell observed that law "comprises both legislative enactment and administrative ruling. For it is clear that power resides in both, the administrative and legislative functions—both are participants in the decision-making process."[6] In the Western world, the administrative branches succeeded some time ago in carving out for themselves a political hegemony thriving on the elements of complexity, technicality, and scope. In a case such as the one before us, the end result may be identical—administrative hegemony over legislative function—but for different reasons.

In addition, the legislative function in Nigeria is affected by the following factors, among others: (1) Only a relative handful of civil servants and lawyers command the requisite skill to comprehend legislation, its purposes and scope, and are capable of translating it into appropriate administrative directives. (2) The possibilities of error in the drafting, printing, interpreting, and applying of legislation are so great that it would be advisable at times, in the interest of effective and efficient management, for the administrative function to take precedence. (3) The basic laws are so inadequately codified, so beset with amendments—more often than not, entirely makeshift—so alien in conception and form to local culture and precedence that very few Africans can hope to acquire legislative expertise in the foreseeable future—unless the entire structure is torn up by the roots and a new beginning is made, which clearly would not be much of an improvement since the other factors, of course, would still apply. (4) Where traditional authorities are in control of regional and local administration, the police, and the courts, administration rather than legislation is the instrumentality of power. Through administrative fiat, law is applied there to maintain the status quo.[7]

In terms of political stability, as in other respects, the welding of the legislative, administrative, and judicial functions—which is the rule in the north—would appear to have the greatest value. The legislative function in the north, however, if examined by itself, does not display the systematic development required for the ultimate acquisition of intrinsic value in the political stability complex. Unless rescued from the limbo in which it has been placed by British colonial practice, and from which it has not been moved by the Anglo–Northern Nigerian elite now controlling positions of power, it will further atrophy under the impact of the inevitable difficulties accompanying the transfer of power from colonial to wholly indigenous control.

While on the subject of law, it might be noted that essentially the same problems besetting the legislative function in government and administration confront the entire legal structure down to the lowest court and enforcement office. It will be a very long time before concepts like "constitutionality" and "legality" can be applied seriously, consistently, and universally throughout Nigeria. The administrative machinery, in terms of available skills, personnel competence, and numbers, will be far too inadequate and insecure to permit anyone in authority to examine too closely and too objectively the legal processes, unless it is the purpose of such an examination to create confusion and doubt. Where misinterpretation, clerical procedural, and judicial error are the rule, authorities intent on maintaining stability, and on increasing the prestige of governmental institutions, will wisely refrain from encouraging procedural inquisitions. In fact, they will discourage an insistence on perfection. On the strength of direct personal observation, one may suggest that most court cases contain at least a few technical errors that could be employed to invalidate proceedings or to create confusion. Insistence on legal and procedural perfection could well lead, therefore, to legal chaos under such circumstances. Groups interested in political instability, and in social instability, for that matter, are already attempting to bring about such chaotic conditions by immersing local authorities (which are more vulnerable) to massive litigations, challenges, and appeals.*

Opinion-Making

If one assumes that the rulers and the supporting bureaucracy are capable of perceiving the policy needs of the several regions and of the federation, the question arises whether or not they possess the skills to communicate and to direct the population toward accepted, generally beneficial policy goals. This question relates to literacy and education, to the availability of competent "opinion-makers," articulators, or systematizers, as Lasswell designates them, and to the fields of propaganda, public relations, and advertising.

The major sources of difficulty confronting government agencies in their effort to propagate certain ideas, values, or perspectives, to promote and facilitate their wide acceptance, or to control public opinion toward specific policy goals or political ends are found in these areas:

1. Illiteracy and ignorance. The problem derives from the inability of the audience to perceive the concepts underlying specific propositions (educational or propagandistic) in terms usefully and meaning-

* Prosecution of such a campaign, during the 1959 federal and several regional elections, constituted a major item in the electoral campaign budgets of the Action Group and the NCNC.

fully related to the original intent. Thus, instruction in certain health practices by means of educational films may lead to conclusions and reactions substantially unrelated to the subject matter, or even detrimental to the entire purpose.[8]

2. Inadequate communication media, diffusion problems, and language limitations.

3. Lack of trained articulators, systematizers, etc.

4. Difficulties experienced by both the disseminator of information and the public in relating alien concepts or political, social, and economic organizations, behavior, and value systems to traditional indigenous concepts and practices.

Hence, it would be advisable to apply caution in attempting to explain the real meaning of a vote in a national or regional election, of parties and of programs, of government in general. Hence, Lerner's question: "How does the enlargement of the opinion arena work out in a society that is not yet genuinely participant, where the bulk of the population still lives in rural illiteracy? Can the leaders short-cut the historic course of modernization by 'involving' their people ideologically before they are involved sociologically?"[9]

The question presses itself upon the analyst of contemporary Nigeria: What will be the feedback from the illiterate masses as the input of information is accelerated in volume, intensity, and complexity? Can the output in terms of social and political action really be predicted? Under the program developed in the relatively advanced Western Region, modern American public-relations devices and methods are employed for both specific and general electoral purposes. It is doubtful that audiences who see the same film several times over and still do not seem able to grasp its message—for example, the proposition that mosquito control is best achieved not by measures against witchcraft but by cutting the bush back—will comprehend and properly translate a political message received on radio, TV, film, or in a speech given by a man who "descends from heaven" by helicopter.[10]

It would appear that the organization of public opinion for certain specific goals is favored greatly in areas of relative social stability, such as the north. There Islam provides a fabric that is sufficiently tight to facilitate relatively efficient communication through the familiar and traditionally legitimized channels (a significant source of political power at the disposal of the northern rulers and one which they guard jealously). There the goal must of necessity be that of preserving the status quo because the communicators, the systematizers, and the audiences share an interest in that respect—the audiences, however, only because they know of no other goal or status as yet. Revolutionary ideas could hardly be communicated through these channels. Thus, in the north, political stability could conceivably be enhanced through molding public opinion, provided that the concepts communicated are in line with general expectations and are disseminated through accepted channels. Backing up the communicators are the multitudinous agencies of Islam and the supporting feudal society and governmental machinery; in addition, the native police and customary law and practice are all brought into play in an attempt—albeit a losing one—to keep the channels open and subversive ideas out.

To a less rigorous extent, similar practices can be observed in the southern regions. At least, an attempt is being made there to enforce uniformity, encourage defenders of the dominant idea system, and interfere with disseminators of undesirable oppositional ideas. Here too, customary law, land-tenure leverage, patronage, and police action are utilized. But at all times, traditional concepts, images, and values are marshalled to communicate what is required to mobilize support for the policy goals of both the government and the western or eastern regional authorities. Economic power is tapped to buy the talents of the opinion-makers in the local communities—the scribes, extroverts with communication skills of sorts, the story tellers, praise singers or minstrels, persons of prestige, members of royal families, bearers of symbolic value, etc. Where traditional rulers, the *obas*, have maintained a significant part of their influence and prestige—although, as indicated above, this is on the wane—they are utilized by the rulers, political parties, or other manipulators of political power. The relative freedom of action found in the more mobile and more open southern regions, especially in the west, favor oppositional groups and, hence, competition. To utilize traditional channels of communication undisturbed becomes, of course, more difficult under these circumstances.

The major difficulties remain for the propagation of ideas not supporting the status quo. It is extremely doubtful that progressive elements acting within the general framework of legal-constitutional restraints will be able to mobilize the masses toward policy goals with revolutionary implications. The masses will not comprehend in the manner intended, will not react as expected; moreover, defenders of the status quo will have at their disposal numerous channels open only to them, which they control—monopolize, in fact—and may manipulate at their pleasure. Thus, progress probably cannot be achieved wherever mass support is required without the introduction of numerous elements of compulsion.

Yet, such an attempt could itself be frustrated in the communication sector. To reduce this handicap, and to achieve a semblance of stability, it would be necessary to subdue and then to control all conflicting communication channels, including those of a traditional nature.

Opinion-Casting

Does Nigeria possess an adequate number of persons skilled in the art of systematizing political thought and practice, concepts of government, and social and political ideological propositions and myths? Are the personnel available to formulate practical ideas for holding society together in the coming difficult times? And if so, who are they? For purposes of a stability index, only those elements are considered here that can be expected to be effective in a modern setting, the assumption being that Nigeria, to move forward, must embrace new concepts, new idea systems, and new practices. Should the traditional, feudal, and regressive northern rule spread throughout Nigeria, then the *malams*, scribes, etc. would of course suffice.

Under conditions determined within the legal-constitutional system governing Nigerian politics at the time of independence, the only systematizers of the official political idea system were the expatriates, a few African journalists, and a handful of academicians. Many of the latter were themselves too deeply involved in partisan politics or in the broader politics of transition—which frequently center on who fills which position left vacant by departing colonials—to devote much time to the production of treatises, tracts, or even pamphlets. The few journalists who devote themselves to the extremely delicate and politically unhealthy subjects of power politics, rule, and political ideology may be classified as systematizers; but most others, of minimum capabilities, such as returned students, are economically too weak, psychologically too insecure, and politically too immature to produce anything of impact or of lasting value.[11]

At independence, the Western Region had used, and the Eastern Region planned to use, television. It remains to be seen whether the receptivity of the Nigerian audiences, the mass segment primarily, improves with that new medium; whether the personnel will be available to assure adequate utilization of the medium, and of radio, theater, and motion pictures for the constructive or even merely effective manipulation of public opinion. For a long time to come, a large part of the communication personnel will have to be foreign and thus will be unsuitable for politically delicate communication and control purposes.

Security

From the beginning to systematic, area-wide Western rule to independence, the governing security concept has been that of the colonial regime. It has had as its primary goal the protection and defense of the imperial interest against internal and external threats. Given the conditions of what then, for all intents and purposes, was an authoritarian regime, the methods of coercion, persuasion, and control were those of the police state. There was virtually no appeal from the decision of the security forces; the few who could appeal were usually identified with the colonial rulers in one way or another. Even following the turnover of formal power the security services were effectively still under British control.

The rationale for exclusive British control of the security apparatus, the investigatory as well as the executory aspects, should remain valid for a considerable period of time beyond independence. Adequate internal and external security requires a degree of administrative skills that few Africans possess or are likely to develop in the foreseeable future. Those who do command the requisite skills—and again the Western Region has many more qualified persons than the remainder of the country—are normally too committed to other functions to render effective service in this sensitive sector. Given the continued availability of British personnel, the indigenous rulers would be ill advised to tamper with what has proved to be an adequate and efficient security setup. It is, for instance, very difficult to locate in Nigeria today indigenous personnel wholly invulnerable to subversive influences, including pressures from tribal or other associates. Furthermore, the concept of *total* security is not at all developed in Nigeria, but it is only fair to say that it may not be developed in any former colonial areas. One of the main causes of this is the difficulty Africans have in respecting official secrets; the problem seems to be particularly acute when these secrets are, or are believed to be, of value primarily to foreign interests. The problem was expressed rather candidly in an editorial in the Federal Government's *Morning Post* on January 5, 1962, under the heading "Hawking Our Secrets":

> In the days when the British were the indisputable masters of Nigeria, it was the duty of the Nigerian to fight. . . . These were the circumstances in which it was thought that it was not immoral to engage in stealing official documents. . . . We must learn now to real-

ize that it is immoral for our people to engage themselves in stealing government documents, and we must tell those who are supposed to give leadership to the country [i.e., the rulers in the several regions] that they cannot rightly encourage such thefts.

And we cannot but urge our civil servants to keep the terms of their oaths by ensuring that, whatever their private interests and political views, they cannot rightly justify that files entrusted to them should get on to the market place, marked simply, "for sale or for the beloved party."

Because it is becoming the real source of anxiety for all who know the rate at which files go missing, the rate at which secrets of governments are published, and the ease with which anybody seeking any information to which he is not even entitled can get it—all from official sources without official sanction.

For an independent nation, this is ominous.

No less candid was the remark by the Federal Minister of Finance in Parliament when discussing certain data related to his Ministry: "These are all facts that could be checked in my Ministry and in the Accountant-General's office where expatriates still are. They are not Nigerians that could be bribed by anybody." [12]

But Nigerianization marches on and demands its sacrifices; certain politicians are especially apprehensive over the continued occupancy by expatriates of positions of high political sensitivity. [13] The resultant pressures, of course, directly countervail the security interests of the regional and federal authorities and of the country as a whole. It might be noticed in passing that substantial numbers of the leaders share the misgivings expressed by the Federal Minister of Finance. Under these circumstances, it is very difficult to give the Nigerian security services a high stability rating. Normally, venality, corruption, and untidiness are incompatible with security. The incompatibility is greatest where the penetration of the security machinery has a high pay-off value, where information to be gained is worth the risks involved in its unauthorized procurement. In the Nigerian case, the risks attending penetration of a sensitive agency are few because of the administrative weaknesses referred to above. To cite but one illustration: In most of the sensitive offices there exists no reliable system of filing and document-accounting; hence, the removal of a document may not be noticed until it is required, and even then far too many alternatives exist to explain its absence to permit firm conclusions to be drawn on the subject.*

From Bush to School

A Colonial Office memorandum of February, 1954, outlined the central political and functional theme of Britain's educational policies in Africa as follows: "[African Education] must develop qualities of citizenship and the capacity for self-government; it must provide training in all the various skills and techniques which a self-governing nation needs; and it must give its people an understanding not only of the potentialities of their own country, but of the essentials of Western Culture."[14] There was, of course, little or no doubt in the minds of the authors of that statement that the attainment of these goals, or even of a reasonable facsimile thereof, lay in the distant future. At any rate, self-government came to Nigeria, first to the two southern regions, and then to the north, long before the goals had been sighted, let alone attained. A quantitative evaluation of the educational achievements aside, Nigerian educational levels are qualitatively very low. British insistence on the highest standards and correspondingly restrictive, highly selective admissions policies at secondary and higher levels did not help. On the eve of independence, Nigerian institutions of higher education had not yet materially re-

---

* The present writer was filled in on the details of a case which may serve as a prototype: The Northern Regional Government, to support its case before the *Commission to Enquire Into the Fears of Minorities* in 1958, prepared a "Red Book." For security reasons, only a limited number were printed; each copy was numbered, and all were to be strictly accounted for. On the decisive day, by sheer coincidence, one of the expatriate representatives of the northern regime glanced out the window of his cottage and discovered the bright shining copy of his government's "Red Book" in the hands of a representative of the opposing Western Regional Government. He retrieved the copy. When, subsequently, the attorney general's office in the north began to investigate the matter, suspicion was drawn to a printer of southern tribal identity. At the decisive moment, the records pertaining to this man's activities and involvement in the case were removed from the office by a fellow tribesman.

duced the country's dependence upon outside sources of skilled manpower. Crash programs planned in the 1950's and 1960's may, in time, produce needed cadres of technicians and of certain types of administrators. The effect of unbalanced crash programs on political and civic training, however, cannot be anything else but negative. It may be pointed out that the educational policies of the British Administration in Nigeria, as elsewhere, have not been particularly imaginative; standards have been applied to Nigerian schools that had been developed under wholly different cultural conditions. Moreover, British standards had been applied in a manner far more rigid than had ever been the case in the home country, primarily for want of alternatives acceptable to the overseas administration.[15] An examination of the curricula at the primary and secondary school levels at independence revealed a poverty of references to the local Nigerian environment and to the social and political facts of life in an African country. If the Nigerian student perceived any significant social or political problems, those were, more likely than not, problems related to the British Isles. He remained singularly uninformed about the governmental and political problems of Nigeria unless he was able to exchange colonial environment for the freer, more liberal, and politically more sophisticated American or French metropolitan climate.

In terms of the creation of significant educational foundations for self-government, the mission schools, with too few exceptions, and the northern system of Koranic schools have been particularly ineffective, even harmful. Although both types provided some elementary—one might say, primitive—social skills, neither dared or cared to approach subjects directly relevant to the training of good citizens in a self-governing Nigeria, unless one considers the superficial Koranic training in the northern Islamic schools adequate preparation for participation in the feudal political system there.*

---

* This is not saying that the mission schools could have provided these services against the wishes of the secular authorities and, incidentally, against the wishes and policies of their own superiors in the home countries.

Aside from the problems of standards and content, there are the problems of the impact of the product of the educational processes of society. *West Africa,* commenting on the expected output of Western Regional schools under the free education program there, noted that by December, 1960, over 200,000 boys and girls, the first under the program, were expected to leave the schools. This was to be compared with only 60,000 the year before. The other regions were expected to face the same or a similarly increased output later. "In the end," the periodical comments, "independent Nigeria's greatest domestic problem may prove to be the employment of her school-leavers." [16] Similarly, the country, as is most likely true of any developing society, will be hard pressed to find adequate outlets for the output of the universities, once these begin to operate under new policies—policies developed, perhaps, along the lines of the massed efforts characteristic of the United States. The need for trained and educated people can of course not be denied in Nigeria. The question here is to what extent education can be pushed ahead without adverse results in terms of political stability. Will the products of free primary education go back to the farms? What will their expectations be? How will their social and political perspectives be affected by their educational experiences? Likewise, what will be the social and political roles of the Nigerian university products who are studying or graduated? There can be no doubt that they will exert pressure on government. One critical element in the problem complex is the ability of the country to create a machinery and a program for the systematic utilization of the educational product. Because most young Nigerians were trained in what for local, social, and political purposes may best be described as a vacuum, any politically potent and stimulating information rushing into that vacuum from outside, whether from sources in the East or the West, the Communist countries or the United States, and regardless of the methods and means by which this is accomplished, will have unsettling effects. The manner in which non-Nigerian methods are being injected into the educational bloodstream—for example, in the new university in eastern Nigeria—is not uniformly confidence-inspiring. The West may be emulating the sorcerer's apprentice.*

The foregoing, of course, is addressed to short-range effects. Improved educational programs should lead the citizens to improved participation in the political processes. It should ultimately raise the capabilities of the people to evaluate more effectively, and in their own interests, the performance of their governors. Where government is of high caliber, this should have positive effects; but because of the pronounced weaknesses among the rulers entrenched at the time of, and immediately following, independence, any realization of these weaknesses by a growing segment of the public, especially by students, could have unsettling, unstabilizing results.

The question arises whether or not the channelling of newly generated energies toward socially desirable goals can be accomplished in the social and political framework of Nigeria operating at the time of independence. The women in the north, who are, with few exceptions, denied the benefits of education, will be integrated in time, but what will be the impact of female education on the social positions allocated to them under Islamic rule?

Generally, youth must be directed or redirected into channels compatible with the developmental goals of Nigerian society. For a considerable time to come, they cannot be allowed to browse among subjects of convenience at universities, or to select careers primarily advantageous to them individually or to their families. Can this be achieved within the democratic system? If not, what modifications must be made in the system to secure the full benefits of educational and training programs? If foreign enterprise is permitted to compete with government for the services of the highly trained and highly skillful, what will be left to government? In other words, one of the prime questions confronting the post-

---

* It is too early to assess adequately the value and contribution made to Nigerian education by the several United States private foundations and organizations. Their motives certainly are above reproach.

independence government in the sphere of education and its impact on political stability is that of the management of the end product during the difficult period of transition. Indications available at the time the country attained independence were not encouraging.

In the fall of 1960, a commission under the chairmanship of Sir Eric Ashby published its report on higher education in Nigeria. For present purposes, the most significant aspect of the proposals was that there was little hope of implementation unless Nigerian education became for the time "an international enterprise." It is also of significance that several proposals indicated the commission's conclusions: that the several regional governments lacked the determination and resources to implement the educational plans required to permit Nigeria to move toward needed goals in the coming twenty-year period.[17]

Old Concepts, New Habits

It is doubtful whether many Nigerians perceive the link between their own individual and group welfare and political stability. For the overwhelming majority of Nigerians, federal and regional government represent abstractions that are perceived only in the barest and vaguest outline, if at all. Although no representative sample was taken by the present writer, spot checks indicated no real comprehension of governmental relationships, no perception of social and political dimensions, no consciousness of the individual-society nexus.[18] The traditional ways and concepts are of little help to the individual in this respect. Under conditions of rapid change, most of the social and spiritual guideposts provided by the traditional systems are in danger of losing utility value. Fundamental differences between traditional and modern systems require fundamental human adjustments.

If, by systematic, carefully conceived planning, modern government and society are meaningfully related to, and integrated with, selected aspects of traditional government, traditional attitudes

and perspectives might, to a modest but psychologically significant degree, recover utility value for the individual. Of some relevance here might be the observations contained in the World
Bank Report on the Nigerian Economy:

> Other Nigerian social traditions have positive value in a period of
> rapid change and advancement. Respect for Elders and their coun-
> cil, if not carried to the point of becoming an impediment to learning
> new ways, make for social restraint and stability.
>
> Respect for learning in any form and the authority enjoyed by
> *mallams*, "learned men" in the north, and by teachers, professors, and
> even students in the south, suggest the key role which the teaching
> profession can play in developing new attitudes and in the adoption
> of new institutions and techniques.[19]

It is debatable, of course, whether a working and truly meaningful relationship can and should really be established. So far,
where attempts in that direction have been made in Lagos, they
appear not to have advanced beyond purely superficial identification for formal, ritual purposes. In the Northern Region, of
course, where traditional rule is still dominant, the situation is
quite different; there, traditional attitudes and perspectives do
have social validity and political value, as long as the traditional
rule maintains its hold in the region. As has been noted elsewhere,
conflicts do appear to be forming even there: for instance, between the perspectives of elected officials and hereditary rulers
and their supporters.

One immediate consequence of the aforementioned problem
relates to the means to be employed by the state to provide services
and, in general, to stimulate growth and advance. Because of a
fundamental lack of understanding of the goals, purposes, and
structure of the modern state, too many businessmen fail to
understand the need for private initiative, private risk-taking, and
self-help. Although even in advanced societies, such as the United
States, the relationship between taxes and government services is
not always fully understood, too many Nigerian businessmen demand all conceivable services and repudiate their obligations to

pay taxes or to accept increases in existing ones. Likewise, the need for private and group initiative is not understood by those who deplore graft and corruption in hospitals, in the produce-inspection service, in industry and private business. Perhaps because of their previous reliance upon the colonial administration and because of the corresponding lack of participation in political and economic decisions, businessmen in the post-independence period will probably not develop the sense of inter-relationship between themselves and their own government. Consequently, the integrating, promoting, developing, and stimulating functions of economic agents in the new Nigerian society cannot be relied upon to contribute to the stabilization of the political and social structure as taken over from the colonial power. To the contrary, increasing pressure will emanate from this direction in favor of a greater centralization and expansion of government responsibility in the economic sector. It could be that prevailing economic practices cannot be relied upon by either a central or decentralized system because of the manifest lack of cohesion.[20]

It appears to be a widespread belief among those engaged in economic pursuits that the government is not *their* government but someone else's. This tends to interfere with their capabilities to contribute effectively to the stabilization of conditions in Nigeria. The Economic Report continues: "The heavy reliance on government is frequently coupled with a strong distrust of its actions and motives. To some extent this is explicable as the response of a people still under tutelage and exposed to the complexities of Western civilization."[21]

What under one set of conditions may appear to have stability value proves, under different conditions, to have the opposite effect. For instance, the behavior patterns and social and moral perspectives—in fact, the entire value system associated with traditional society—operate against political participation and integration in a modernizing society for the following reason: They promote clannishness, conflicts of loyalty and morality. The concept is widespread, all-pervading in fact, that the loyalty and morality adhered to within the family and the clan do not apply to strangers. This can be observed vividly in court proceedings, where witnesses feel obligated to lie to the stranger in the judge's chair to protect the interests of clan or family. It has been noted, for instance, that many Nigerians operate under a nearly total disregard of personal rights and private property, seemingly because there is no recognition of these concepts outside of family or clan. Contractual obligations are disregarded or given a very low value wherever personal or group interests countervail, because a contract with strangers does not have the same force as an undertaking within the family group. It is not hard to imagine what impact attitudes of this kind have on political relationships or how they will affect the concepts of political representation.

Where traditional perspectives and values have lost their validity and modern society has not yet developed a framework for the full integration of the individual and group, not only is the level of civic responsibility likely to be nearer the critical point but stability no longer is a matter of concern to the citizen.

Customary gifts and corruption require special consideration in an evaluation of political stability. It should, of course, be understood that customary gifts do not necessarily reflect corrupt practices. However, where adapted to modern conditions, especially conditions of rapid economic growth, the practice of giving and receiving customary gifts imperceptibly enters the twilight zone between courtesy and corruption. Because corrupt practices, including those traditionally associated with tribal government, permit the more powerful to exact tribute from their subordinates, it encourages social injustice and, hence, creates conditions conducive to social-revolutionary activities. Secondly, because the practices generally described as an exchange of customary gifts are widespread throughout Nigeria and are well established historically, it is most difficult for the general public to regard them as anything but normal. Consequently, the public tends to regard the evils flowing from those practices as normal and necessary. Thus, an exchange of gifts and presents in conjunction with a promotion, an appointment to administrative positions, or support at the courts in judicial proceedings, if viewed as normal and treated as a legitimate social practice, tends to obscure the more positive, socially significant, and wholesome aspects of government and administration. They certainly interfere adversely with the development of healthy popular perspectives concerning the purposes and functions of government and administration. Where such conditions prevail, cynicism, apathy, and ingrained opposition to authority are likely to become accentuated.[22]

Several consequences of corruption in its modern forms are worth noting. In a country with inadequately developed channels of communication and transportation, it is easier to bypass legal, institutional, and procedural channels and obtain results more quickly and satisfactorily. Under such circumstances, a likely goal of anyone seeking advantage or advancement is to seek influence through bribery. Competition sets in among those offering bribes, and both the giver and the receiver soon regard this method as the most reliable and effective one. There are innumerable signs throughout Nigeria, notwithstanding valiant efforts to the contrary, that economic, political, and social survival is more and more assumed to depend upon one's ability to offer, to solicit, and to receive bribes.

Another consequence is the diversion of talent from serious study, of value to society, to socially less constructive, although personally more rewarding, pursuits. A factor in this is the fear that prolonged study and training may foreclose opportunities for the quick accumulation of wealth; the acquisition of political influence, under those conditions, appears to be a more desirable goal and a more direct road to success than university training consuming seven years or more of one's lifetime. In Nigeria, which still suffers from a lack of adequately trained administrators of top-level quality, this is a serious matter.

The focus on corrupt practices as a means of improving one's position partly results from the fact that a considerable gap exists between the living standards of the masses and those of the few on top. Also, opportunities for legitimate private employment, respectable by Western standards, are still relatively few and unrewarding if compared with the fruits of corrupt practices. The rewards expected from such practices, under these conditions, appear to be far greater than those available in more advanced and economically more diversified societies. Also, since a very substantial segment of the ruling elite has become party to these practices, it is most difficult to institute reforms.*

Still another effect upon political stability derives from the range and intensity of domestic political influence acquired by foreign commercial and industrial firms seeking to overcome the handicap of their late arrival by resorting to corrupt practices. Concentrating on the more extensive and more lucrative opportunities offered by governmental and public authorities, they find that bribery often is the only key to success. Because of the large sums involved, some of these firms begin to eclipse many of the less adequately financed, hence politically less potent, local interests. But the idealists among Nigerian nationalists object to their country's wealth being squandered, misdirected, and subverted.

What are the main sources of these problems (1) The lack of precedent for public and private functions, responsibilities, roles, and practices. Frequently, it is impossible for a newly established businessman, or an employee of a government agency, to determine for himself proper or improper procedures, legitimate or

---

* One of the most lucrative areas for corrupt practices appears to be that of construction and development in general. It is standard operating procedure for firms seriously bidding for contracts to locate key personnel in government at all levels and to offer bribes. It is generally recognized that major contracts cannot be obtained without bribery. Competition among firms from Britain, Germany, Italy, etc. only increases the degree of corruption. Fewer and fewer firms are prepared to leave their business interests up to chance and to rely solely on the merit of their bids. Businessmen and investors may have to consider that in order to stay in business, or to have a fair chance of success, it may be necessary to calculate into the cost the expenses of bribery. On the other hand, conditions may have reached the point in some sectors of commerce and industry where ministers, and the government generally—at both the federal and regional levels—may re-evaluate the situation to determine whether it is wise to permit businessmen to be pressed beyond the point of financial prudence as well as of endurance.

illegitimate. (2) The absence of a generally recognized code of ethics. Christianity and Islam have not yet arrived at a working understanding in Nigeria in this or any area. (3) The absence of an aroused public opinion, or of a public sufficiently aware of the practices and, more important, of their social implications (4) The inadequate supervision by the highest authorities. The British, in the waning days of colonial rule, were reluctant to alienate Nigerian politicians and businessmen, except where they had reason to believe that such supervision was politically expedient—for example, the aforementioned case against the then Premier of the Eastern Region, Dr. Azikiwe. (5) The availability of large sums of money for corrupt purposes, and the differential gap between available remuneration for legitimate pursuits and gains obtainable through corrupt practices. (6) The absence of enforceable penalties that would render corrupt practices sufficiently unpleasant for all but the most skilled and most determined. Under favorable circumstances, it may require only a modicum of capital, and sometimes not even that, to commence accumulating wealth. A position in a key office in the government may be all that is required to become an affluent member of society, for all the risks may be assumed by the party interested in obtaining the official's favor. Under these conditions, the observance of established formal rules and procedures to effect political change is not materially encouraged.

Going Through the Motions: Voting

Too many observers of the political processes in developing areas regard voting for political offices as a matter adequately assessed by the quantitative measurement of official election tallies. If viewed in this fashion, electoral behavior in most countries in Africa appears to be substantially not unlike that in advanced countries; Africans seem to perform their roles reasonably well, depending upon the area and administrative level under review. Voter participation is represented in percentage points, which are usually quite impressive, ranging from below 50 per cent in some parts to close to or even over 90 per cent elsewhere. If one accepts the maxim that high voter participation is the essence of democracy—"Vote as you please, but vote!"—Nigeria, with a voter participation in the 1959 federal election of 79.8 per cent would appear to be quite "democratic." If viewed differently, however, the picture is less reassuring.

In the first place, the rate of literacy in the politically controlling part of the federation, the north, is about 2.7 per cent. In the federation as a whole, it is no higher than 15 per cent. These figures show the extent of the communication problem in relating, or attempting to relate, the voting function to the remainder of the political and governmental complexes. Secondly, there is strong evidence that the secrecy of the vote is not yet sufficiently accepted and observed by all concerned. The author had occasion to examine the specially designed polling structures—one cannot call them "booths"—that were in use in the north during the 1959 federal elections and in local northern elections subsequently. It was apparent to voters and officials alike that it was not at all difficult to observe the casting of the ballots and, in particular, to determine how the vote was cast, from certain positions outside the flimsy, roofless structures. One observer, speaking of elections in the north in 1961, put the matter quite succinctly: "One thing, however, was obvious—the system of voting could scarcely be described as secret." [23] This pattern appears to be prevalent throughout the country, and it would seem that it is far too early to interpret election results in an area like Nigeria in terms of the "will of the people."

In the third place, tallies of votes cast are rarely accurate; the degree of inaccuracy and carelessness, in some instances, mounts in direct proportion to the distance of the polling place from the national or regional capital. One British election official, commenting on election results and the accuracy and reliability thereof, noted: "One gets some results of sorts. Someone will bring in a sheet of figures, scrawled in many instances and sometimes blurred to obliteration by rain or perspiration. Many report sheets never arrive at headquarters. They are lost on the way." Fourth, since the administration of elections in Nigeria is still in its infancy, voters, officials, and tallies are ready prey for corrupt practices. Fifth, the overwhelming majority of the voters are still vulnerable to influences wholly extraneous to the electoral processes.[24] Sixth, if regarded as the "key mechanism of consensus in democratic society," voting in Nigeria is far less effective than might be deduced from studies of poll-participation figures. Lipset stresses the "integrative aspects of electoral behavior," and his observation that "a system in which support of different parties corresponds too closely to basic social divisions cannot continue on a democratic basis" is also of relevance here.[25] In Nigeria, most political action on the popular level is not likely to reflect much beside tribal loyalties or relatively petty local grievances. Under such conditions, the electoral processes cannot be expected to perform much of a socially integrative function at this time.

The conceptualization of the voting process also requires close analysis—much closer than has generally been undertaken by Western observers—for it is unlikely that the voter is capable of visualizing either his own role or the relationship of his voting to the democratic representative function and to the executive functions that flow from it. The depth of the individual voter's attachment to the principles of democracy also needs to be more fully evaluated. This writer, during a sample-pilot survey in 1959, arrived at the tentative conclusion that only a modicum of pressure is required to divert the majority of Nigeria's voters from democratic to antidemocratic or authoritarian preferences; and that since no substantial values are attached to the voting privilege, it could readily be replaced by other functions more of a ceremonial, ritualistic, and traditional nature.[26]

As has been noted above, the opinion appears to be widely held that for Nigerians, and Africans in general, traditional institutions and practices have sufficient training value to assist them in their adjustment to modern secular democracy. This appears to be a wholly unrealistic view. Traditional and secular democracy have wholly different social frames of reference, totally different values; modern democracy tends to diffuse individual perspectives to the point where the individual, particularly the illiterate and uneducated one, loses sight of them and consequently becomes detached from the political process. What may have been active participation under traditional rules becomes passive participation in the modern diffused setting. It is submitted here that the traditional systems for selecting chiefs or headmen have little bearing on the Nigerian's ability to become a fully conscious participant in modern democracy. As has been noted by Coleman, the role of the chief can readily be translated into something more modern, but not necessarily something more democratic.[27]

In the electoral problem complex, there is no real substantive consensus of opinion among Nigerians on fundamental issues of national import. There are only aggregates of views of a predominantly parochial nature, ranging from views on village and clan affairs to tribal and regional matters. It is doubtful whether regional matters are comprehended and treated as such or are not really local issues inappropriately related by Western observers to affairs at higher levels. If there appears to be a consensus during an election campaign, it is usually based on reports and evaluations haphazardly and uncritically conducted. Most important, what appears to be opinion consensus may be merely the ephemeral reaction of the public to efforts by uniformity-producing media such as newspapers, radio, speakers, and now television, for the apparent identity of views disappears as soon as the issue has been superseded by another. The survey cited above indicated that political opinions are most likely no more than superficial reflections or responses and that the slightest counterstimulant quickly leads to a substantial alteration of views. For example, questions on dictatorship, or dictatorial tendencies among candidates or parties, often elicit answers that reflect not only a superficial comprehension of the issues and implications but a superficial attachment to the principles endorsed by the respondent. Dictatorship that was "bad" or "undesirable" becomes "good," or "desirable" if the question is only slightly modified. Dictatorship is given a negative value if it is represented as interfering with individual rights, but a positive value if represented as conveying stability, unity, and peace.[28]

At the time of independence, internal political behavior in Nigeria lacked the element of cohesion required of any society for reasonable longevity and sustenance. There was only superficial attachment to issues, preferences were echoed but not personalized, and expectations of such matters as independence were so wholly illusory as to lack all practical value. The criteria for judging leaders, candidates, and office holders were incompatible with the requirements laid down in constitutions. For example, the expectation of largesse being distributed by the chief, a traditional practice, is extended to the secular leader as well. The rules of the political game are not adequately understood, or, perhaps better, they have not yet been formulated to the satisfaction of a substantial segment of the population.[29]

Going Through The Motions: Talking*

As in the case of voting behavior, parliamentary behavior is too frequently misrepresented as a function of notable achievement in terms of purely formalistic, mechanistic performance. In most instances, this is done without the benefit of data or evidence related to the substance of that function, either representative, legislative, deliberative, or informational. It is done without any real investigation of the feasibility of parliamentary institutions in the country. It is done only with a view to the presence of persons seated in a certain order, following certain formal rules, speaking to each other in a reasonably well-disciplined manner, and being associated, in one form or another, with "legislative output." It is also noted, as if it mattered, that officers wear cer-

---

* A distinction is made between legislative function, discussed earlier in this chapter, and parliamentary behavior, although the former tends to influence the latter.

tain costumes or garments and that the chambers feature certain regalia and equipment reminiscent of older, proven institutions of similar purpose.

Is a tough interchange between the men in power and their would-be supplanters possible in the African context? Much of the foregoing would indicate that parliamentary institutions patterned after Western models may not be appropriate for Nigerian purposes. A growing number of observers begin to recognize the inadequacy of Western parliamentary practices in the African setting. It might be predicted that the Nigerians will find ways, in spite of a seemingly tight constitution, to do away with them. Because of the precarious balance among the three major parties operating in Nigeria at independence, the retention of many, if not most, of the formal aspects of parliamentary government as practiced under colonialism, was, of course, recommended. That balance is ephemeral, though, and much more than a temporarily expedient accommodation is required to make parliaments meaningful and valuable as a governmental device.*

Legislatures throughout the world are in decline, including the House of Commons, and attempts to saddle Nigerian legislative houses with responsibilities long ago abandoned or committed to disuse in the "mother of parliaments" would not seem to be fair. Of course, parliaments still perform some significant functions, provided that certain conditions are met. For example, there must be effective and politically meaningful personal links or liaison between the members of parliament and the effective rulers of the country. In Nigeria, such links exist only in an exceedingly small number of cases. The overwhelming majority of members of all parliaments, federal and regional, are not significantly con-

---

* For those, and this includes the author, who especially appreciate the brilliant display of humor in West African parliaments, it might be worth realizing that humor wanes where the economic and social struggle turns serious. To most members of the Nigerian parliament, federal or regional, at independence, the seriousness of their situation had not yet become a reality. Cf. Leonard Doob, "The Psychological Pressure Upon Modern Africans," *Journal of Human Relations* (Spring–Summer, 1960), p. 472.

nected to centers of power of any kind; they may more appro-
priately be described as cogs in the parliamentary machinery,
expected to perform primarily ceremonial functions that they are
taught to perform but that they do not entirely comprehend. As
yet, too few opportunities exist to enable individual politicians to
attain positions of financial, hence political, independence. Political survival chances for those intent on opposing government,
and the ruling elements in particular, on fundamental issues are
rather slim.* Secondly, what applies to administration in general
applies also to the parliamentary processes. Too few of the members of the several parliaments comprehend the vast and constantly changing implications of what is formally placed on the
agenda. It might be said that parliaments in the Nigerian setting,
as in all countries in analogous stages of development, resemble
the ancient Roman galleys, where every member of the crew is
expected to contribute his ounce of strength, in unison and in
accordance with the prescribed rhythm, toward objectives that
none would fully comprehend even if made privy to the top-deck
strategic decisions.[30]

The deliberative function of parliamentary processes at times
assumes promising proportions, but only if one were to overlook
the fact that constructive contributions are made by a mere handful. The Senate appears to be in a better position than the House
to engage in constructive, truly deliberative debate. Alas, the
Senate has no power. In the Federal House of Representatives,
the Public Affairs Committee does a fairly impressive job in ex-
amining the operations of the government and in bringing instances of waste, corruption, and mismanagement at least to the
attention of the legislators. The leader of the Opposition, Chief
Awolowo, at times performs brilliantly in the role of principal
critic of the coalition government—aside, of course, from inevita-

---

* Compared to the citadels of governmental power and prestige, only the
British, some other foreign business interests, and exceedingly few Nigerians
appear to command an adequate counterforce to ward off retaliatory measures
in the power struggle.

ble lapses into political party propaganda. But many an incisive comment or significant revelation is quickly submerged, mainly by those adversely affected, in a welter of vehement, wholly irrelevant, partisan recriminations and plain, unabashed heckling.

As for the informational function of parliament, far too few of the members of the several houses in the country are interested in, or capable of, performing as informational or educational media for the benefit of their constituencies. It is more likely that, upon contact with their electors, they will attempt to belittle what in their estimation has been a rather frustrating and, in terms of what *they* deem to be the most important issues, irrelevant experience. This is true, most of all, of those parliamentarians who expect from the legislative processes legal production rather than general debate. Those who view parliament primarily as a propaganda forum should be quite elated. As the battle for existence is joined more decisively among the contending parties and groups and as the superficial but temporarily ameliorating British influence wears off or is discarded, the informational function of parliament will be reduced even further. Candid and frank conveyance of the substance of parliamentary discussions in Lagos, under certain conditions, may be deemed subversive activity in the north, perhaps everywhere, except in Lagos.*

* If Parliament in Nigeria today fails to perform significant functions, it should be pointed out that this is not the fault of the Speaker of the House, who fights the deterioration valiantly if unsuccessfully.

Conclusion

The reader may ask why so critical an analysis has been written at a time when Nigeria appeared to be the lodestar of Western democracy on the strife-torn continent of Africa; when that large, potentially wealthy, and well-populated country seemed to carry the hopes of the free world for stability in an area of increasingly strategic importance. So that there may be no misunderstanding on that point, let it be said that the present writer has immense confidence in the ability of the people of Nigeria, of many of their leaders, and of many of the Europeans still guiding affairs ultimately to overcome the handicaps that have been pointed out in this book. One motivation for the book was the author's fear that conditions conducive to enabling the people of Nigeria to achieve a substantial improvement of their lot were not being created, partly because the basic problems confronting the country were not understood abroad, partly because a new myth of wishful thinking had been born in response to the political and ideological requirements of the Cold War. The new myth mistakes the community of interests between the leading Western countries and a group of Nigerian rulers oriented toward the status quo for a valid formula to cope with Nigeria's problems. It was felt that it would be in the best interest of the Nigerian people —and, incidentally, also of the West—if an analysis was prepared to clear the air of false assumptions, of intellectual cobwebs spun in the days of colonialism, and of local applications of fallacious and self-defeating Cold War propaganda.

Another purpose of this book was, of course, related to the study of political behavior in developing countries. It was believed that the two purposes could be brought conveniently together in the theme of political stability.

In conclusion, the foregoing study isolated, analyzed, and evaluated several social, economic, and political indices of direct relevance to the state of affairs described as political stability. It was found that the positive factors are outweighed by negative factors, resulting in the constancy of political instability, no matter what type of system should prevail. Because the steps being taken by the former colonial power, Great Britain, by the Nigerians themselves, and by other powers, including the United States, must of necessity be long-range propositions with regard to their maximum effectiveness, and because the political requirements for stability are short-range and immediate, current and projected development plans, although impressive, are unlikely to stave off social-revolutionary pressures building up as the developmental gap widens inexorably.

Reduced to generalizations, the problem-complex of political stability in Nigeria may be summarized as follows: Historical and environmental conditions, geared to strongly centralized, authoritarian government characteristic of colonial regimes, breed instability wherever decentralization and the general loosening of restraints are substituted. The social and political ideas, perspectives, and value complexes that developed in the traditional and the colonial setting are substantially irrelevant and immaterial for modern purposes. Although the adaptation of aspects of traditional society may be feasible, such an adaptation must coincide with substantial changes in other sectors of society. The effective rulers reflect the interests of expatriate groups and of indigenous groups dedicated to the perpetuation of conditions here assumed as being unacceptable to an ever-increasing segment of the masses. At the same time, the effective rulers, depending for their survival upon forces on their way out of the political arena, are also removed from the centers of effective control by the very decentralization that they and the departing colonial power devised together. Attempts at seizure of the central agencies of the federal system by members of the counterelite are a constant possibility; but such a seizure of power would not by itself bring stability to Nigeria. The stability value of the effective rulers is further reduced by their dependence upon factors under foreign control such as capital, skilled technical personnel, and the management of key sectors of society, economy, and policy.

The substance of the political arrangement under which Nigeria became independent may be summarized by the terms moderation and compromise. But Nigeria, it is submitted, already has entered a period of social-revolutionary pressure and upheaval. Moderation and compromise on essentials, on fundamentals, under such conditions, are least likely to produce political stability. All that may be achieved is a postponement of unrest, riot, and a general showdown among the principal contenders for power. It is vitally important to the development of Nigeria that temporary tranquility is not mistaken for a solution of Nigeria's problems; it should not even be allowed to be represented as a valid base for future solution of basic problems. At best, a policy of moderation and compromise serves the political Cold War interests of the West in the narrowest possible sense. Real progress toward lasting stability in Nigeria requires, among other things, the separation of Cold War objectives and stratagems from the real social and political engineering problems awaiting solution for their own sake.

Appendix

Note on the Technique of Interviewing in Nigeria

As indicated earlier, some interviews conducted in conjunction with the foregoing study were of an experimental survey type. It is felt that the experiences gained in this particular study—even though it is not unique—may, in all likelihood, be of value to researchers; therefore, the most significant items of information are presented here in the form of a brief explanatory note.

In the surveys, two major objectives were pursued: one related to the perception of political concepts and relationships generally; the other, to role-perception and functional problems in political-party structures. The first objective was general and entered into research, open-ended and personal interviews, and surveys in all the major regions and several subregions of Nigeria. The second included the core of a survey conducted among Action Group functionaries in Ibadan, Western Region.

Both surveys were not only experimental but also of a random nature, restricted not only by lack of funds but also by other factors, some of which become apparent from the following: Since the environment is novel to most researchers, partly because it is non-Western, partly because conditions are primitive and difficult, it is suggested that questions be subjected to a dry run prior to the full application and expenditure of large sums of money. It is doubtful whether all difficulties can be fully anticipated without such a test. It goes without saying that questions should not be phrased without adequate consideration of local conditions; thus questions related to income or to social and economic aspects that are, in turn, related to income may evoke responses quite different from those in a Western setting. Several questions of the kind asked in the first few houses in a village may effectively preclude any further investigation there because of a general suspicion, which quickly travels ahead of the surveyor, that questions are designed to facilitate the work of the tax collector, the census taker, and the police. No amount of certification can completely eliminate this hazard.

It is doubtful whether significant answers can be obtained without elaboration, elucidation, and explanation of the terms used. Likewise, it is doubtful whether several sets of answers to a given set of questions can really be evaluated without a simultaneous evaluation of the comprehension factor. It is unlikely, for instance, that any appreciable number of villagers in the bush will have the same or reasonably similar concepts of electoral processes, party organization, and government. Thus, the safeguards and checks found in the better questionnaires employed in Western countries may have to include different kinds of checks that probe deeper. In the work done by the present writer in both surveys, it quickly became evident that respondents had varieties of concepts about political-party activity. Although they used terms like party, party headquarters, canvassing, elections, registration, and so on, they appeared to be thinking about a variety of relationships and activities ranging from parties to social associations, from business and trading objectives to tribal associational activities. They also appeared to have only the vaguest ideas concerning divisional and jurisdictional responsibilities within parties.

Where a knowledge of the language is required, it should be kept in mind that it is not enough for the interviewer to be proficient in translating questions, for he must be able to translate and interpret the terms used in the questionnaire into terms with which respondents can be expected to be familiar in the vernacular. Extreme caution will, of course, have to be applied in this regard if explanations and supplementary information are introduced. Yet it may be entirely unwarranted to assume that a given respondent knows what the term "election campaign" means, even though he may manifestly be playing a part in it. This writer is now inclined to take little for granted in that respect in Africa.

Yet, while many more checks and safeguards may have to be

built into the questionnaire in non-Western areas, the document
should not be too long and the application of it not too time-consuming. Although the assumption may appear to be warranted
that in the relatively leisurely African environment, unhurried and
relatively free of the kind of social and economic pressures in advanced societies, lengthy questionnaires and extended question-
ing periods may not be objectionable, the contrary seems to be
indicated. First, the respondent attaches a special value to the
time spent with the interviewer; even though he may have no
responsibilities whatever preceding and following the session, he
may nevertheless seek to convey the impression that he is a rather
busy person. An extended interview will clash with this principle
and, beyond a certain point, materially reduce the value of the
product. Second, the respondents are likely to tire easily from
mental effort; this is especially so if inner tensions are built up by
the interview, a very likely development in nearly all instances in
Africa. To assure a relaxed atmosphere, the interviewer may have
to prepare himself and the subject far more extensively than may
be required in advanced societies. Thirdly, and somewhat related to the foregoing, the interviewer must endeavor to become a
familiar sight in the environment in which he intends to operate.
His motivations must be "telegraphed" not only to his research
targets but also to persons likely to influence the targets, if only to
reassure all concerned. Some locally acceptable rationale for the
exercise must be current in the geographic area in which the interviews are to be conducted. It would not be adequate, however,
if only the respondent, but not the group of which he is a part,
knew of the rationale. Although the individual respondent may
find the interviewing acceptable and trust the interviewer, the
group of his associates may view the exercise with suspicion, in
which case fears and misgivings of the group will be transmitted
to the respondent from outside. Thus, although politically non-
sensitive questions may elicit equally harmless answers, the group
of which the respondent is a part may view his participation with
distrust and may, in fact, draw conclusions about the respondent's

loyalty to the group. The next respondent, consequently, may already be adversely influenced before the interviewer reaches him.*

A source of considerable difficulty may be the interviewer himself, especially if he is an African. In the Ibadan survey, the principal interviewer was a student from Ibadan University, an institution that was then suspect among Action Group functionaries because of its known sympathy for the principal opposing party, the NCNC. He was also an Ibo, which made matters even more difficult because the Action Group is primarily composed of Yorubas. The student had been recommended to the writer by a person closely identified with Dr. Azikiwe, then the leader of the NCNC. This made him further suspect. The fact that one of the principal Action Group functionaries made a point of inquiring specifically about the tribal origin and source of recommendation of the interviewer to be employed in the survey of lesser functionaries of that party is in itself revealing. Thus, the person of the interviewer, in the Nigerian setting and probably throughout Africa, can easily become a major factor, influencing the outcome.

Control of the interview in the Nigerian setting is impeded by many additional factors not necessarily of significance in advanced societies. Thus, much depends upon the image produced by the exercise in the respondent's mind, aside from the references made earlier. There is the feedback danger, a hazard well known to surveyors in advanced societies, where the telephone can raise havoc with community responses. In the Nigerian setting, it was found that a community attitude forms much more quickly than may be suspected in a telephone-less environment. Some respondents clearly sought time to consult whoever had to be consulted before they were prepared, or authorized, to provide replies. Their requests for a one-day delay or for several hours in many instances was believed frequently to have been motivated by a desire to

---

* A Nigerian official in the Federal Census Office, commenting on the reliability of census figures in the Western Region, suggested that "among the Yoruba it is an article of faith not to tell the truth to a stranger."

check with the consensus of local opinion concerning the propriety or legitimacy of the project and the nature of their own
likely responses. In several instances, a certain respondent among
those interviewed appeared to have been designated by the group
to present the "official" reply to certain questions. Many respondents evidently were set for certain questions and frequently
primed with answers as well; some respondents wanted time to
consult with persons already interviewed to compare points in the
interest of group unanimity.

Inquiries into political behavior in Nigeria, as perhaps in most
of Africa, are especially fraught with danger, because there the
political processes are too closely linked to the participant's social
and economic existence. Too many questions, which are quite
safe in advanced Western societies, are extremely delicate and
sensitive in the Nigerian setting. Thus, questions concerning political relationships may nearly always touch upon vital economic
relationships; economic influence is frequently social, and political
influence is nearly always social. The individual is embedded too
firmly in the web of authority to permit him to strike out on his
own; therefore, he cannot successfully detach himself from the
web and all that this implies about his future and his personal
security. Political processes, in other words, are central, not
marginal, issues in most instances; in advanced societies, it would
be the other way round.

A social problem appears to exist in the sector of political-
party functionaries, for party organizers in the Ibadan setting
seemed to regard surveying as a kind of espionage, aside from the
problems posed by the tribally and politically unacceptable interviewer. They feared that party workers would, or could, be
trapped into revealing information that normally they would not
reveal to anyone—particularly the following: (1) Strategic information concerning the party's fortunes. (2) Tactical and organizational information of value to opponents. (3) Any revelation that
party workers would view as rendering them vulnerable to retalia-
tion by hostile political forces, which would impair their effective-

ness to the party. (4) Improper, illegal, or otherwise objectionable activities that, although deemed necessary for victory by the party command, might be left unexecuted if party workers gained the impression that they would be held to account for their acts by outsiders who trapped them into confessions during a complicated interview. It might be pointed out, in that connection, that the suspicions and fears of the party command in this and other instances should be treated with much sympathy; clearly, the level of intelligence and literacy of party functionaries in that setting is rather low, and the consequences of a survey, however carefully conducted, could bear out the stated fears.*

* A few annotations made by the interviewer in the Ibadan survey may be of interest here: "It was very difficult to interview this man, who did not understand most of the questions. He was, however, quite enthusiastic." "One woman offered the interviewer five shillings because she loved her party so much that she was 'grateful to anyone who discussed something good about the party' with her." "Some respondents were quite enthusiastic and appeared to be greatly honored." "This respondent was extremely calm and most thoughtful in his answers. He thought at least five minutes before he answered any questions."

Notes

Preface

1. James S. Coleman, *Nigeria: Background to Nationalism* (Berkeley, Calif.: University of California Press, 1958).
2. For instance, Gabriel Almond and James S. Coleman, *Politics of Developing Areas* (Princeton, N.J.: Princeton University Press, 1960).
3. Harold D. Lasswell and Abraham Kaplan, *Power and Society: A Framework for Political Inquiry* (New Haven, Conn.: Yale University Press, 1950).

Chapter 1: The Roots of the Prevailing System

1. Lord Hailey, *An African Survey* (rev. ed.; London and New York: Oxford University Press, 1957), p. 453.
2. See Coleman, *op. cit.,* pp. 25 ff.; Hailey, *op. cit.,* p. 465. Murdock notes: "States of considerable magnitude occur among the Edo, Igala, Igbira, Ijaw, Itsekiri, Nupe, and all tribes of the Yoruba cluster, but elsewhere, political integration does not transcend the level of the local community." G. P. Murdock, *Africa: Its Peoples and Their Culture History* (New York: McGraw-Hill Book Co., 1959), p. 248.

Chapter 2: Westminster: Export Model

1. The House of Representatives had passed an amendment to the Constitution of the Northern Region that would have permitted the Grand Khadi, a Moslem lay judge (but learned in Islamic law), to sit in a panel with Judges of the Regional High Court. This move was interpreted by non-Moslem elements as being a step preliminary to introduction of Islamic legal concepts and practices at the federal center; see Federation of Nigeria, *Parliamentary Debates,* House of Representatives (hereafter cited as *Hansard*), 1961–62 session (November 23, 1961), cols. 3367–79.
2. Taylor Cole, "Emergent Federalism in Nigeria" (unpublished paper).
3. Great Britain, Colonial Office, *Summer Conference on African Administration* (Publication No. 1178, 1951), pp. 7–8.
4. James Griffith, *ibid.,* p. 14.
5. *Ibid.* See also L. Gray Cowan, *Local Government in West Africa* (New York: Columbia University Press, 1958), p. 65; F. Tannenbaum, "On Political Stability," *Political Science Quarterly,* LXXV, No. 2 (June, 1960), pp. 160–80.
6. See Margery Perham, Colonial Office, Summer Conference, *op. cit.,* p. 20.
7. See Cowan, *op. cit.,* pp. 6 ff.; Hailey, *op. cit.,* pp. 453 ff.
8. Cowan, *op. cit.,* p. 65.
9. *Ibid.,* p. 77.
10. Colonial Office, Summer Conference, *op. cit.,* p. 93; see also The Royal Institute of International Affairs, *Nigeria: The Political and Economic Background* (Oxford: Oxford University Press, 1960), pp. 66–67.

Chapter 3: Values and Ideas

1. Lasswell and Kaplan, *op. cit.*, p. 25.
2. *Ibid.*, p. 261.
3. Cf. Seymour Lipset, *Political Man* (New York: Doubleday and Company, 1960), p. 61: "Economic development, producing increased income, greater economic security, and widespread higher education, largely determines the form of the class struggle, by permitting those in the lower strata to develop longer time perspectives and more complex and gradualist views of politics."
4. The case of Dr. N. Azikiwe, presently Governor-General of the Federation, provides a good illustration; see Great Britain, *The Report on the Inquiry into Allegations of Improper Conduct by the Premier* (Eastern Region, Nigeria), Cmnd. 51 (London: Her Majesty's Stationery Office, 1957).
5. See Cowan, *op. cit.*, pp. 131 ff.
6. *Op. cit.*, p. 76.
7. *Ibid.*, p. 83.

Chapter 4: Effective and Ineffective Rulers

1. *Hansard,* House of Representatives, 1960–61 session (November 22, 1960), col. 276.
2. *Op. cit.*, p. 39.
3. Cowan, in G. M. Carter and W. D. Brown, *Transition in Africa* (Boston: Boston University Press, 1958), p. 51.
4. Hailey, *op. cit.*, p. 788: "In the Northern Region of Nigeria the political authority of the Emirs is manifested chiefly in their claim to ultimate control over the land and in the exercise of seigneurial rights."
5. See A. J. Loveridge, "Chiefs and Politics," *Journal of African Administration,* XI (October, 1959), 201–7; for an incisive analysis of the problems of adaptation of the chieftaincy to modern conditions, see J. Gus Liebenow "The Chief in Sukuma Local Government," *JAA,* XI (April, 1959), 84–92.
6. Cf. Chief O. B. Akin-Olugbade, *Hansard,* House of Representatives, 1961–62 session (November 16, 1961), col. 2926.
7. George H. T. Kimble, *Tropical Africa* (New York: The Twentieth Century Fund, 1960), I, 533–34.
8. See the remarks by the Hon. Waziri Ibrahim, *Hansard,* House of Representatives, 1961–62 session (November 22, 1961), cols. 3235–36.
9. The Federal Minister of Economic Development, *ibid.* The Minister noted that "the expatriate firms and individuals who engage in our country's distributive trade and road transport business are extremely powerful, influential, and virtually control the economy of our country. . . ." He also indicated that it would be very difficult to do anything about that aside from "research and surveys." On another occasion, the Federal Minister of Commerce and Industry noted: "The economy of our country, strictly speaking, is not in our hands. Over 70 per cent of our overseas trade is controlled by forces over which we have no control." *Ibid.,* (November 16, 1961), col. 2943.
10. See the debate on a motion to nationalize basic industries, *ibid.,* (November 29, 1961), cols. 3526–88; also *ibid.,* (November 16, 1961), cols. 2895–2907 and 2935–41; and *ibid.,* (November 20, 1961), col. 3128.

11. Sen. Orizu, *Hansard*, Senate, 1961–62 session (March 30, 1961), col. 315; also Mr. Ukaegbu, *ibid.*, House of Representatives, 1961–62 session (November 29, 1961), col. 3568.

12. A rather acid comment on Anglo-Nigerian collaboration was made in a debate in the Senate by Senator Orizu: "The trend now is to call every Company a Nigerian Company. That is, somebody is appointed from outside, a Nigerian, one foolish man, who is usually given a big appointment, and a big salary, so that they can call the Company Nigerian. He has nothing to do with the Company." *Hansard*, Senate, *loc. cit.*

13. A bitter attack against the Syrian and Lebanese businessmen was made by S. A. Ogedengbe, *Hansard*, House of Representatives, 1961–62 session (November 16, 1961), col. 2936.

14. Hugh H. and Mabel M. Smythe refer to the Nigerian business group as "in no sense of the term [forming] an economic power elite." They also note, however, "its influence is increasingly being felt, especially in the political sphere." *The New Nigerian Elite* (Stanford, Calif.: Stanford University Press, 1960), p. 85. See also their "Subgroups of the New Nigerian Elite," Duquesne University, *Institute of African Affairs*, No. 5 (1960), esp. pp. 7–8.

15. Chief Awolowo, Leader of the Opposition, made this comment on the subject in the course of a debate:

"Practically all the major and minor extractive and secondary industries within the country, and the bulk of our shipping business, as well as of our commercial undertakings . . . are in the hands of foreigners.

"By various intricate and subtle devices these foreigners exercise an effective monopoly over our economy.

"Because they control the bulk of our financial institutions, they accordingly influence, for good or ill, the availability . . . of adequate capital and credit and their eventual direction." *Hansard*, House of Representatives, 1961–62 session (November 29, 1961), col. 3527.

16. Federation of Nigeria, *The Economic Development of Nigeria: Report of a Mission Organized by the International Bank for Reconstruction and Development at the Request of the Governments of Nigeria and the United Kingdom* (2nd ed.; Lagos: Federal Government Printer, 1954), p. 10.

17. This conclusion is based on personal interviews in all regions; the author was seeking to discover why qualified persons failed to compete or apply for higher political or administrative posts.

18. Evidence to that effect was offered by a substantial number of community leaders in selected constituencies in the three regions.

19. David Apter, *The Gold Coast in Transition* (Princeton, N.J.: Princeton University Press, 1955).

20. Daniel Lerner (ed.), *The Human Meaning of the Social Sciences* (New York: Meridian Books, 1959), p. 32.

Chapter 5: The Working Elite and the Enemy

1. *Daily Times*, October 6, 1959, p. 7.

2. Information regarding Nigerianization and related subjects may be located in the following sources, among others: Federation of Nigeria, *Report of the Commission on the Public Services* (Lagos: Federal Government Printer, 1955); Federation of Nigeria, *The Nigerianization of the Civil Service*

(Phillipson Report) (Lagos: Federal Government Printer, 1954); *Federation of Nigeria, Views of the Government . . . on the Interim Report of the Committee on Nigerianization,* Sessional Paper No. 7 of 1958 (Lagos: Federal Government Printer, 1958); Federation of Nigeria, *Final Report of the Parliamentary Committee on the Nigerianization of the Federal Public Service,* Sessional Paper No. 6 of 1959, and the government commentary on this report, Sessional Paper No. 2 of 1960 (Lagos: Federal Government Printer, 1959 and 1960, respectively). (See also note 4 below.)

3. Cf. the suggestion made in the recommendations of the Harragin Commission to the effect that the Senior Service may be regarded as a specially created social elite for purposes of providing political stability in a socially, and politically, vacuous situation, and the suggestion advanced by a member of parliament that the Senior Service therefore might be regarded as a kind of wooden horse left behind by the departing colonial rulers. *Hansard,* House of Representatives, 1960–61 session (November 22, 1960), col. 276.

4. See Federation of Nigeria, *Matters Arising from the Final Report of the Parliamentary Committee on the Nigerianization of the Public Service: Statement of Policy by the Government of the Federation.* Sessional Paper No. 2 of 1960 (Lagos: Federal Government Printer, 1960), p. 4. See also a most thoughtful paper, leaning toward a contrary evaluation of the problem complex, by J. Donald Kingsley, "Bureaucracy and Political Development with Particular Reference to Nigeria," *Conference on Bureaucracy and Political Development* (Stanford, Calif.: Center for the Advanced Study in the Behavioral Sciences, 1962).

5. Secretary of State's dispatch of February 25, 1947, as quoted in Colonial Office, Summer Conference, *op. cit.,* p. 45.

6. Cowan, *op. cit.,* p. 67.

7. In Carter and Brown, *op. cit.,* p. 50.

8. On local government and political parties, see Cowan, *op. cit.,* p. 232.

9. Federation of Nigeria, Sessional Paper No. 6 of 1959, *op. cit.,* p. vi: "The Committee has come to the irresistible conclusion that the two Nigerian Higher Institutions of Learning are contributing very little to the solution of man-power problems and problems of Nigerianization of the Public Service."

10. At least one stinging attack was made in the House of Representatives against United States, British, and other foreign advisors, professors, technicians, etc. It was suggested that these people were subversive and had been sent to prepare the ground for further exploitation. It was alleged that this applied to "medical, technical, religious, and legal aid," and that "educational interests cannot be completely divorced from economic interests." R. O. A. Akinjede, *Hansard,* House of Representatives, 1961–62 session (November 18, 1961), cols. 3028–32. Numerous veiled criticisms of the employment of foreign advisors have been made in both houses. For an evaluation of Nigeria's manpower needs, see Frederick Harbison, "High-Level Manpower For Nigeria's Future," in Federal Ministry of Education, *The Report of the Commission on Post-School Certificate and Higher Education in Nigeria* (Lagos: Federal Government Printer, 1960), pp. 50–72. (Ashby Report.)

11. *Op. cit.,* p. 265.

12. Great Britain, *Report By The Nigeria Constitutional Conference, May–June 1957,* Cmnd. 207 (London: Her Majesty's Stationery Office, 1957), pp.

29–30. The military and police leadership elements are considered separately below.

13. In response to criticism that the Army has not been Nigerianized rapidly enough, the Federal Minister of Finance observed: "We do not want to promote a Sergeant to a Lieutenant or Captain the next day, just because we are independent. You know what has resulted from this. You want to produce Mobutus here to overthrow all of us." The Hon. Okotie-Eboh, *Hansard*, Senate, 1961–62 session (April 20, 1961), cols. 588–89. The Nigerianization of the police had progressed by April, 1961, to this extent:

	Expatriate	Nigerian	Total
Commissioners	5	—	5
Deputy Commissioners	6	1	7
Assistant Commissioners	14	4	18
Senior Superintendents	34	2	36
Assistant Superintendents	153	287	420

SOURCE: *Hansard*, Senate, 1961–62 session (April 26, 1961), cols. 543–44; and Nigerianization Division, Federal Establishment Office, Lagos; see also Sessional Paper No. 2 of 1960, *op. cit.*, p. 22 for data on Northernization of the police.

14. While discussing the Nigerianization of the police, one member of Parliament commented: "The trend that things are taking at the moment does not appear to give any hope to the idea that the indigenous Police Force which we are hoping to evolve will be a good Police Force." Sen. Asemota, *Hansard*, Senate, 1960–61 session (May 2, 1960), col. 452; also *ibid.*, col. 465.

15. For a debate on the political and legal implications of a federal TV service, see *Hansard*, House of Representatives, 1961–62 session (November 22, 1961), col. 3239.

16. "There are provinces with a population of 1.5 million and yet we have got only one doctor." The Federal Minister of Health, *Hansard*, Senate, 1960–61 session (November 28, 1960), col. 203. There were a total of 974 Medical Practitioners registered in Nigeria in 1960. *Nigeria Year Book*, 1961 (Lagos, Apapa: Times Press, 1961), p. 87.

17. By February, 1962, there were a total of 170 Nigerian officers in the Army and some 35 in the "pipeline." There were 9 Nigerian commissioned officers in the Navy. *Morning Post*, January 5, 1962, and *Hansard*, House of Representatives, 1961–62 session (November 21, 1961), col. 3139.

18. *Op. cit.*, p. 266.

19. *Op. cit.*, p. 93.

20. *Op. cit.*, p. 264.

21. In its most vexing dimension, the problem was succinctly formulated by a representative of expatriate interests in the Senate, Sen. L. C. Daldry: "The main domestic policy of any Nigerian Government, must be to raise the standard of living of the people . . . this means that imports must continue to rise. . . . And this is the main economic problem in Nigeria now—how to raise the living standards without allowing imports to become too high." *Hansard*, Senate, 1961–62 session (April 26, 1961), col. 547.

22. Cf. R. J. Molard, *Afrique Occidentale Francaise* (Paris: Editions Berger-Levrault, 1956), p. 87.

23. J. Spencer Trimingham, *Islam in West Africa* (London and New York: Oxford University Press, 1959), p. 209; Sir Abubakar Balewa, while a member of the Northern House of Assembly, was identified with that orientation. See Northern House of Assembly, *Reports,* August 19, 1950, cols. 91–98.

24. Trimingham, *op. cit.,* p. 210.

25. Much of parliamentary debate in both Houses during the first year of independence was devoted to this topic. See especially *Hansard,* House of Representatives, 1961–62 session (November 29, 1961) cols. 3526–88.

26. *Ibid.,* cols. 3527 and 3538 respectively.

27. In 1953, well before independence, the British Government had obtained assurances from the regional leaders not to employ Communists in their regional services. Federal Minister of Commerce and Industry, *Hansard,* House of Representatives, 1960–61 session (November 29, 1960), col. 567. Other measures to contain Communism included travel restrictions to Eastern Bloc countries, restrictions on the operation of Soviet missions, and a ban on Communist literature. The ban was lifted in November, 1961, but the Federal Prime Minister warned at that time: "We shall not hesitate to use our power under section 58 of the Criminal Code . . . if we find that our faith has been misplaced and that this sort of literature directly threatens the security of the State or the sovereignty of the country." *Hansard,* House of Representatives, 1961–62 session (November 22, 1961), col. 3232.

28. The Federal Minister of Finance intimated that the NYC had received financial aid from Ghana and "Eastern" countries. *Hansard,* House of Representatives, 1961–62 session (November 18, 1961), col. 3018. Concerning several speeches by the President of the Congress, the Federal Minister of Internal Affairs warned: "The Government is really alive to what is happening and is aware of the statements the gentleman has been making. I would like to assure the House that Government will not allow, under any circumstances, any single person . . . to incite people against any individual or any constituted authority." *Ibid.,* (November 27, 1961), col. 3520. The principal objection appears to have been to allegations of corrupt practices by named Ministers, but it is clear that the Federal Government would like to proceed as drastically against its critics as the several regional regimes are accustomed to doing.

Chapter 6: Groups: Popular Kaleidoscope

1. *Op. cit.,* p. 36.

2. *Op. cit.,* p. 31. Lipset continues: "A system in which the support of different political parties corresponds too closely to basic social divisions cannot continue on a democratic basis, for it reflects a state of conflict so intense and clear-cut as to rule out compromise. Where parties are cut off from gaining support among a major stratum, they lose a major reason for compromise."

3. *Economic Development Nigeria* (1954), *op. cit.,* p. 10. The report recommended that "full support should be given to the cooperative movement as a vehicle for economic development, for it is a form of economic organization fully compatible with Nigerian tradition and social sentiment."

4. *Op. cit.,* p. 154.

5. *Op. cit.,* p. 307.

6. The potentially explosive nature of the religious relationships in the Federation was alluded to when a member of the House of Representatives demanded censorship of news broadcasts by the Nigerian Broadcasting System. In particular he expressed fear that inclusion of news on religious conflict during the 1960 presidential campaign in the United States would trigger similar conflicts in Nigeria. One such broadcast over the Nigerian system was described as "religious warfare with American elections." Mr. Akwinu, *Hansard*, House of Representatives, 1960–61 session (November 23, 1960), col. 333.

7. Cf. Taylor Cole, "The Independence Constitution of Federal Nigeria," Duke University Commonwealth Studies Reprint Series, No. 6 (reprinted from *The South Atlantic Quarterly*).

8. In November, 1961, the House of Representatives adopted a Resolution to "introduce the teaching of Hausa, Yoruba, Ibo, and other languages into institutions of learning throughout the country with a view to adopting one of them as our official language in the near future. . . ." This was not likely to be realized for a variety of reasons, one of which was reflected in the following comment by a member of the House: "If we try to impose any language, whether it is Hausa, Yoruba, Edo, or Ijaw on the rest of the country we will be establishing a new imperialism." Chief Enahoro, *Hansard*, House of Representatives, 1961–62 session (November 21, 1961), col. 3158. The debate on the motion brought to light a wide range of objections as well as arguments in favor; see cols. 3145–78.

9. On April 26, 1961, the Senate passed a resolution, previously passed by the House of Representatives on April 4, to establish a fourth region within the Federation, generally designated as the Midwest Region. *Hansard*, Senate, 1961–62 session (April 26, 1961), cols. 488–500. The relevant constitutional documents are listed in the bibliography to the present volume.

10. Nigeria, Northern Region, *The Penal Code Law, 1959* (Kaduna, Northern Region: Government Printer, 1959); Northern Region, *Statement by the Government of the Northern Region . . . on the Reorganization of the Legal and Judicial Systems of the N.R.* (Kaduna: Government Printer, 1958). Although, on paper, basic human rights are guaranteed in the north as well as in the rest of the Federation, it is generally accepted that the legal reforms notwithstanding, the northern regime still operates along feudal lines. A careful study of the Federal Constitution's civil rights provisions reveals that they are so thoroughly circumscribed and hedged as to permit almost any practice, including slavery. See *Hansard*, Senate, 1960–61 session (May 3, 1960), cols. 513 ff. and 546. On slavery and forced labor, see Great Britain, Statutory Instruments, West Africa, *The Nigeria (Constitution) Order in Council, 1960,* chap. iii (Fundamental Rights), sec. 19.

11. Nigeria, Eastern Region, *House of Chiefs in the Eastern Region*, Eastern Region Official Document No. 1 of 1959 (Enugu, Eastern Region: Government Printer, 1959). Eastern Region, *Report of the Position, Status, and Influence of Chiefs and Natural Rulers in the Eastern Region* (Enugu, Eastern Region: Government Printer, n.d.). Western Region, *Local Government Manual* (incl. Chiefs' Law, 1957) (Ibadan, Western Region: Government Printer, 1957).

12. *West Africa,* November 22, 1958, p. 1115.

13. Federation of Nigeria, *Report of the Constituency Delimitation Com-*

mission, 1958 (Lagos: Federal Government Printer, 1958), p. 9. The Commission reported that they deliberately avoided drawing constituency boundaries in accordance with tribal boundaries. They noted: "accurate ethnic boundaries are usually very hard to draw owing to the gradual mixing of different ethnic groups in the areas where they come into contact with each other. When considering these conflicting interests, we have usually decided to prefer administrative rather than ethnic boundaries, on the grounds that the inconvenience that would be caused by crossing the administrative boundaries outweighs the merits of the representations made to us. . . . In all cases where boundaries are not involved and the size of constituencies is not compromised, we have tried to include people with a community of interest in the same constituency."

14. Thomas Hodgkin believes it to be misleading "to describe African townsmen as 'detribalized,' for in many respects tribal and kinship ties remain strong," *Nationalism in Colonial Africa* (New York: New York University Press, 1957), p. 81.

15. See P. C. Lloyd and K. W. Post, "Where Should One Vote?" *Journal of African Administration,* XII, No. 2 (April, 1960), 99–104.

16. In 1958, the total force of employed workers amounted to no more than 2 per cent of the population of Nigeria. J. I. Roper, *Labour Problems In West Africa* (London: Penguin Books, 1958), p. 16. Cf. the comment by Stephen Low that "membership, however, is a poor measure of union strength in this part of the world. A union with a handful of members has been known to bring out 30,000 workers on strike for over a month." "The Role of Trade Unions In The Newly Independent Countries Of Africa" (Unpublished paper presented at the Research Seminar On Comparative Labor Movements, Washington, D. C., September, 1960), p. 9.

17. Jules Weinberg commenting on Stephen Low's paper, *ibid.,* p. 18.

18. Thus, the over-all finances of over 200 trade unions in Nigeria were estimated, in November of 1960, to be about $8,000 Sen. Chief O. A. Fagbenro-Beyioku, *Hansard,* Senate, 1960–61 session (November 28, 1960), col. 213. Most unions are company unions, some comprising no more than seven members. For an illuminating debate on the strength and weaknesses of the Nigerian trade-union movement, see *Hansard,* House of Representatives, 1960–61 session (November 26, 1960), cols. 509–27. The occasion was the debate on the government-proposed check-off system, the major purpose of which was to render union leadership more secure financially and hence less prone to agitate. *Ibid.,* col. 513. There also was the hope that the check-off system would obviate outside, foreign aid to the weaker unions. *Ibid.,* col. 517.

19. *Op. cit.,* pp. 63–83.

20. In Lagos, in 1946, half of the houses were declared to be unsanitary. Royal Institute of International Affairs, *op. cit.,* p. 72.

21. *Op. cit.,* p. 78.

22. In 1957, of an estimated 10,000 managerial, administrative, and professional employees in Nigeria, over 50 per cent, more likely 70 per cent, were identified with "government service." Nigeria, National Economic Council, *Economic Survey of Nigeria,* 1959 (Lagos: Federal Government Printer, 1959), table 2E.

Chapter 7: The Way of Doing Things

1. Sessional Paper No. 2 of 1960, *op. cit.*, p. 4. An Organization and Methods unit was established at the federal level in April of 1961 and is now beginning to make its services known within the public service. However, for some time to come this unit will be able to do no more than call attention to proper methods and procedures. The extreme fluidity of the personnel structure alone will frustrate any efforts to bring about substantial improvements, for few public servants of competence remain long in a given slot.

2. The Federal Government's comment is quite revealing: "The Parliamentary Committee's [on Nigerianization] recommendation that everything possible should be done to increase the proportion of Nigerians of northern origin in the Federal Public Service is in accordance with existing policy. . . . "The main difficulty in the matter lies in the fact that an equal need and an equal opportunity for young northern entrants exists at the present stage in the Northern Region Public Service." *Ibid.*, p. 5.

3. *Op. cit.*, p. 592.

4. *Ibid.*, p. 591. Hailey continues: "Where law derives its validity from custom (as opposed to enactment) the conception implicit in the theory of separation of powers of a ruler as law-giver and as judge cannot arise. The authority of the traditional ruler was such that he could secure enforcement of his orders without the intervention of an independent judge." See also M. G. Smith, *Government in Zazzau 1800–1950* (London: Cambridge University Press, 1960), pp. 284–85.

5. Sir H. Maine, cited in Hailey, *op. cit.*, p. 591.

6. *Op. cit.*, p. 196.

7. A salient reference to the problem is found in Hailey, *op. cit.*, p. 590: "Scholars who have sought to define the objective of African customary law, have described it as primarily designed to maintain the social equilibrium, and they have held that the remedies applied for the punishment of offenses or the righting of wrongs were normally seen as a means to restore that equilibrium." Also see J. Keuning, "Customary Law and Customary Court in Western Nigeria," *American University Field Staff: Reports Service, West Africa Series*, IV, No. 6 (August, 1961), Appendix I.

8. P. Morton Williams, *Cinema in Rural Nigeria: A Field Study of the Impact of Fundamental-Education Films on Rural Audiences in Nigeria* (Zaria, Northern Region: Gaskiya Corp., n.d.). Of special relevance here is Leonard W. Doob, *Communication in Africa* (New Haven, Conn.: Yale University Press, 1961).

9. *Op. cit.*, p. 35.

10. Professor M. J. Herskowits appears to be somewhat overly enthusiastic in the following comment made at a United States Senate hearing: "One can never know, but in travelling through Africa, I have been impressed how out in the bush one finds a great deal of interest in political development. This is particularly striking in the case of people who do not know how to read and write, and yet who discuss the problems of their country very intelligently. . . . This interest in politics is reflected in the number of people who vote in elections, a high proportion of them do vote, and all this stems from their

traditional background and interest in political affairs." See U. S. Senate, 86th Congress; Second Session, Committee on Foreign Relations, *Hearings on . . . United States Foreign Policy–Africa* (Washington, 1960), Part I, p. 117.

11. Although the Nigerian press has one of the highest circulation totals, it still was only seven per thousand, and the quality left much to be desired. See Kimble, *op. cit.*, II, 142 ff. Relevant to our purposes may be the observation by Aloba, leading Nigerian journalist, that what is required, among other things, is "patience to wait until telephone exchanges do not keep you waiting for hours to get in touch with your sources of news, and telegrams do not have to go by 30 m.p.h. trains." *Ibid.*, p. 147.

12. The Federal Minister of Finance, the Hon. Okotie-Eboh, *Hansard*, House of Representatives, 1961–62 session (November 20, 1961), col. 3087.

13. Thus, complaints were voiced at the end of the first year of independence that coded messages to and from Nigerian embassies abroad were still being sent via a British controlled cable and wireless system and were being decoded and distributed within the Government by expatriates. Dr. K. Ezera, *Hansard*, House of Representatives, 1961–62 session (November 20, 1961), col. 3128. Also see *Hansard*, Senate, 1961–62 session (March 30, 1961) col. 313.

14. Cited in Kimble, *op. cit.*, II, 119–20.

15. *The Economic Development of Nigeria* (1954), *op. cit.*, p. 364.

16. *West Africa,* September 24, 1960, p. 1070.

17. Ashby Report, *op. cit.*, p. 3.

18. See Doob, *op. cit.*, pp. 365–67, for some data from one of the present author's pilot surveys in Nigeria in 1959.

19. *The Economic Development of Nigeria* (1954), *op. cit.*, p. 11.

20. *Ibid.*, p. 10. "The [economic] mission found . . . Nigerians in all walks of life tend to look too much to the Government, more specifically to the British Colonial officials, for the fulfillment of their aspirations." Also, the mission noted that "the need for self-help is not fully understood by the African businessman who looks to the government, and the government alone, for financial assistance in the expansion of his business. . . ."

21. *Ibid.*

22. Nigeria, Northern Region, *Report on the Exchange of Customary Presents* (Lagos: Government Printer, 1953).

23. "Elections in Sardauna Province," *West Africa,* December 9, 1961, p. 1365.

24. Nigeria, The Electoral Commission, *Report on the Nigerian Federal Elections, December 1959* (Lagos: Federal Government Printer, 1960), p. 12. It should be noted that the Federal Electoral Commission has attempted valiantly, and most skillfully, to raise the level of political conduct. If it has not succeeded, uniformly, it has been through no fault of its personnel. Its tasks have been, and will remain, truly staggering.

25. *Op. cit.*, p. 31.

26. Doob, *op. cit.*, pp. 365–67.

27. *Op. cit.*, p. 328.

28. Doob, *op. cit.*, p. 366.

29. See "Elections in Bornu," *West Africa,* January 2, 1960, p. 10, and "What Nigeria's Voters Think," *ibid.*, November 28, 1959, p. 1029. In this

connection it might be pointed out that many analyses of voting behavior appear to place too much reliance on published manifestos, programs, and policy statements, and appear to assume that a substantial segment of the voting public has seen these sources, has understood them, and has been able to relate them to the voting process. There is very little evidence to support these assumptions.

30. The Minister of State, Dr. Majekodunmi, speaking of the role assigned to the Senate, urged: "We are here to support what the people in the other place [the House of Representatives] had done and we must keep it going whether we are from the West or from the East." *Hansard,* Senate, 1961–62 session (April 25, 1961), col. 483.

Bibliography [*]

Books and Documents

ALMOND, GABRIEL, and COLEMAN, JAMES S. *Politics of Developing Areas.* Princeton, N.J.: Princeton University Press, 1960.

APTER, DAVID. *The Gold Coast in Transition.* Princeton, N.J.: Princeton University Press, 1955.

CARTER, GWENDOLEN M. *Independence for Africa.* New York: Frederick A. Praeger, Inc., 1960.

——, and BROWN, WILLIAM D. *Transition in Africa.* Boston: Boston University Press, 1958.

COLEMAN, JAMES S. *Nigeria: Background to Nationalism.* Berkeley, Calif.: University of California Press, 1958.

COWAN, L. GRAY. *Local Government in West Africa.* New York: Columbia University Press, 1958.

ELIAS, T. O. *Government and Politics in Africa.* London: Asia Publishing House, 1961.

EZERA, KALU. *Constitutional Developments in Nigeria.* London and New York: Cambridge University Press, 1960.

GREAT BRITAIN, COLONIAL OFFICE. *Nigeria: Report of the Commission Appointed to Enquire into the Fears of Minorities and the Means of Allaying Them.* Cmnd. 505. London: Her Majesty's Stationery Office, 1958.

——. *Report by the Nigeria Constitutional Conference Held in London in May and June, 1957.* Cmnd. 207. London: Her Majesty's Stationery Office, 1957.

——. *The Report on the Inquiry into Allegations of Improper Conduct by the Premier* (Eastern Region, Nigeria), Cmnd. 51. London: Her Majesty's Stationery Office, 1957.

——. Statutory Instruments. West Africa, 1960, No. 1652. *The Nigeria (Constitution) Order in Council,* 1960. Supplement to Official Gazette Extraordinary, Nigeria, No. 62, Vol. 47, September 30, 1960.

——. *Summer Conference on African Administration,* Publication No. 1178.

---

[*] In the citations of publications by the Federal Government of Nigeria and by the several ministries and commissions that appear in the Notes and the Bibliography, there are some inconsistencies, reflecting inconsistencies and occasional lapses by the printers in Lagos and London. In order to facilitate a more convenient listing in the Bibliography, the author has identified all materials published in Lagos by or for the Federal Government or other federal bodies under the heading NIGERIA, FEDERATION OF.

HAILEY, LORD. *An African Survey.* (rev. ed.) London and New York: Oxford University Press, 1957.

HODGKIN, THOMAS. *African Political Parties.* London: Penguin Books, 1961. (African Series.)

———. *Nationalism in Colonial Africa.* New York: New York University Press, 1957.

KIMBLE, GEORGE H. T. *Tropical Africa.* 2 vols. New York: Twentieth Century Fund, 1960.

LASSWELL, HAROLD, and KAPLAN, ABRAHAM. *Power and Society: A Framework for Political Inquiry.* New Haven, Conn.: Yale University Press, 1950.

LERNER, DANIEL (ed.). *The Human Meaning of the Social Sciences.* New York: Meridian Books, 1959.

LIPSET, SEYMOUR. *Political Man.* New York: Doubleday and Company, 1960.

MURDOCK, G. P. *Africa: Its Peoples and Their Cultural History.* New York: McGraw-Hill Book Company, 1959.

NIGERIA, EASTERN REGION. *House of Chiefs in the Eastern Region.* Official Document No. 1 of 1959. Enugu, Eastern Region: Government Printer, 1959.

———. *Report of the Position, Status, and Influence of Chiefs and Natural Rulers in the Eastern Region.* Enugu, Eastern Region: Government Printer, n.d.

NIGERIA, FEDERATION OF. *The Economic Development of Nigeria: Report of a Mission Organized by the International Bank for Reconstruction and Development at the Request of the Governments of Nigeria and the United Kingdom* (2nd ed.). Lagos: Federal Government Printer, 1954.

———, ELECTORAL COMMISSION. *Report on the Nigerian Federal Elections December, 1959.* Lagos: Federal Government Printer, 1960.

———. *Final Report of the Parliamentary Committee on the Nigerianization of the Federal Public Service.* Sessional Paper No. 6 of 1959. Lagos: Federal Government Printer, 1959.

———. *Matters Arising from the Final Report of the Parliamentary Committee on the Nigerianization of the Federal Public Service: Statement of Policy by the Government of the Federation.* Sessional Paper No. 2 of 1960. Lagos: Federal Government Printer, 1960.

———, MINISTRY OF COMMERCE AND INDUSTRY. *Handbook of Commerce and Industry in Nigeria.* Lagos: Ministry of Commerce and Industry, 1957 and 1960.

———, MINISTRY OF EDUCATION. *Investment in Education.* Lagos: Federal Government Printer, 1960. (Ashby Report.)

———, MINISTRY OF INFORMATION. *Guide to the Parliament of the Federation.* Lagos, 1961.

———, NATIONAL ECONOMIC COUNCIL. *Economic Survey of Nigeria, 1959.* Lagos: Federal Government Printer, 1959.

———. *The Nigerianization of the Civil Service.* (Phillipson Report.) Lagos: Federal Government Printer, 1954.

———. *Parliamentary Debates,* House of Representatives and Senate. (cited as *Hansard*).

———. *Report by the Ad Hoc Meeting of the Nigeria Constitutional Conference Held in Lagos in February, 1958.* Lagos: Federal Government Printer, 1958.

———. *Report of the Commission on the Public Services of the Governments in the Federation of Nigeria, 1954–55.* (Gorsuch Report.) Lagos: Federal Government Printer, 1955.

———. *Report of the Constituency Delimitation Commission, 1958.* Lagos: Federal Government Printer, 1958.

———. *Report by the Resumed Nigeria Constitutional Conference Held in London in September and October, 1958.* Lagos: Federal Government Printer, 1958.

———. *Views of the Government of the Federation on the Interim Report of the Committee on Nigerianization.* Sessional Paper No. 7 of 1958. Lagos: Federal Government Printer, 1958.

NIGERIA, NORTHERN REGION. *The Penal Code Law,* 1959. Kaduna, Northern Region: Government Printer, 1959.

———. *Report on the Exchange of Customary Presents.* Lagos: Federal Government Printer, 1953.

———. *Statement by the Government of the Northern Region on the Reorganization of the Legal and Judicial Systems of the Northern Region.* Kaduna: Government Printer, 1958.

NIGERIA, WESTERN REGION. *Local Government Manual.* Ibadan, Western Region: Government Printer, 1957.

Nigeria Yearbook. Apapa: Times Press, 1956–61.

ROYAL INSTITUTE OF INTERNATIONAL AFFAIRS. *Nigeria: The Political and Economic Background.* Oxford: Oxford University Press, 1960.

ROPER, J. I. *Labour Problems In West Africa.* London: Penguin Books, 1958.

SMITH, M. G. *Government in Zazzau, 1800–1950.* London and New York: Cambridge University Press, 1960.

SMYTHE, HUGH H. and MABEL M. *The New Nigerian Elite.* Stanford, Cal.: Stanford University Press, 1960.

TRIMINGHAM, J. SPENCER. *Islam in West Africa.* London and New York: Oxford University Press, 1959.

WILLIAMS, MORTON O. *Cinema in Rural Nigeria: A Field Study of the Impact of Fundamental-Education Films on Rural Audiences in Nigeria.* Zaria, Northern Region: Gaskiya Corp., n.d.

Articles and Papers

COLE, TAYLOR. "The Independence Constitution of Federal Nigeria," *Duke University Commonwealth Studies Reprint Series*. No. 6.

DOOB, LEONARD W. "The Psychological Pressure Upon Modern Africans," *Journal of Human Relations*, VIII, Nos. 3 and 4 (Spring and Summer, 1960), 472.

KEUNING, J. "Customary Law and Customary Court in Western Nigeria," *American University Field Staff: Reports Service, West Africa Series*, IV, No. 6 (August, 1961), Appendix I.

KINGSLEY, J. DONALD. "Bureaucracy and Political Development with Particular Reference to Nigeria." Unpublished paper delivered to the Social Science Research Council's Conference on Bureaucracy and Political Development, at the Center for Advanced Study in the Behavioral Sciences, Stanford, Calif., January 29–February 2, 1962.

LLOYD, P. C., and POST, K. W. "Where Should One Vote?", *Journal of African Administration*, XII, No. 2 (April, 1960), 99–104.

LOW, STEPHEN. "The Role of Trade Unions in the Newly Independent Countries of Africa." Unpublished paper delivered to the Research Seminar on Comparative Labor Movements, September, 1960.

SKLAR, RICHARD L. "The Contribution of Tribalism to Nationalism in Western Nigeria," *Journal of Human Relations*, VIII, Nos. 3 and 4 (Spring and Summer, 1960), 407–18.

SMYTHE, HUGH H. and MABEL M. "Subgroups of the New Nigerian Elite," Duquesne University, *Institute of African Affairs*, No. 5 (1960). Reprinted from *Duquesne Review*, November, 1960.

TANNENBAUM, F. "On Political Stability," *Political Science Quarterly*, LXXV, No. 2 (June, 1960), 160–80.

Periodicals and Newspapers

West Africa, 1957–61.
Daily Times, 1959.
West African Pilot, 1959.
Daily Service, assorted issues, 1961–62.
Morning Post, assorted issues, 1961–62.

Index

DATE DUE

FEB 10 '70			
APR 21 70			
MAY 6 '70			
MR 8 '80			
MR 25 '81			
AP 28 '82			
APR 1 6 '86			
MAY 1 '86			
GAYLORD			PRINTED IN U.S.A.